The Heritage
Hiker's Guide
to Hong Kong

PETE SPURRIER

FormAsia

When I began to write the book which became the first in this series – a guide to Hong Kong's high peaks and hiking trails – I had no idea it would lead to the historic walks volume you now hold in your hands.

Even five years ago, there was less call for a book like this. The accepted view was that Hong Kong people cared little for their heritage. Besides the clans of the New Territories, few residents had deep roots in Hong Kong; many had used the city as a stepping stone between China and a more prosperous life overseas. And before the issue of 1997 had been settled, the future of Hong Kong itself was uncertain. Everything was seen as transient. Who would care about a 'borrowed place living on borrowed time'?

Since the protests against the demolition of the Star Ferry pier in 2006, that has all changed. Hong Kong people – and especially young people – have woken up to the value of a connection to their past. Historic places, those which evoke collective memories, now have legions of defenders sworn to protect them at all costs.

This new interest in shared heritage is part of a wider trend towards protest of all kinds: against delays in more representative elections, against reclamation and other harm to the environment, against the profiteering of developers, and most vociferously against the perceived collusion between government and big business. Angry citizens are now ready to confront the government on every issue – a problem the colonial authorities rarely faced. Already it seems that their voices have been heard, and the tide has turned on heritage conservation.

Hong Kong has been many things: a string of fishing villages; a centre of the opium trade; a refuge for revolutionaries; a freewheeling market where fortunes could be made; a prize of war; a window on China; a colony with an expiry date; a beautiful city. It can be hard to find reminders of ages gone by, but they still exist, as these pages will show you. Let this guidebook lead you to discoveries of your own.

Contents

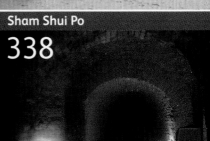

The Peak

Early settlement by Europeans on Victoria Peak was not so much an exercise in avoiding the hoi polloi as a way to escape the summer heat; temperatures on the upper slopes could be noticeably cooler than down below. This is still true, and you can breathe the same rarefied air as those high-society types, and see how they once lived, by following this pleasant route over the Peak and down to the Mid-Levels.

Sedan chair terminus: the Peak Hotel

The Galleria now occupies the hotel's tramside spot

Small beginnings: the first Peak Tram station

Streamline Moderne style for a later terminus

The Peak's cooler climate was of great importance in an age when Europeans wouldn't be seen dead without starched collars or crinolines. Hong Kong thus joined other tropical colonies in establishing a 'hill station' above the city, and wealthy residents started to build mansions up in the clouds. A sanatorium for ailing soldiers was also built in the more comfortable climes. But Old Peak Road, still little more than a wide footpath, was the only way up.

Sedan chair bearers were relieved from their heavy duties in 1888 – a most auspicious year – when a funicular railway opened linking the Peak with Central. The scheme was initiated by Alexander Findlay Smith, who wanted to improve business for his Peak Hotel. **The Peak Tram** was originally steam-driven, with two cars attached to opposite ends of the same cable, and the fare was 50 cents. The front section of the upper tram was reserved for the Governor. The lower terminus on Garden Road has undergone many changes over the years; its current incarnation, **St. John's Building**, is a well known landmark in Central.

All change: today's launching point

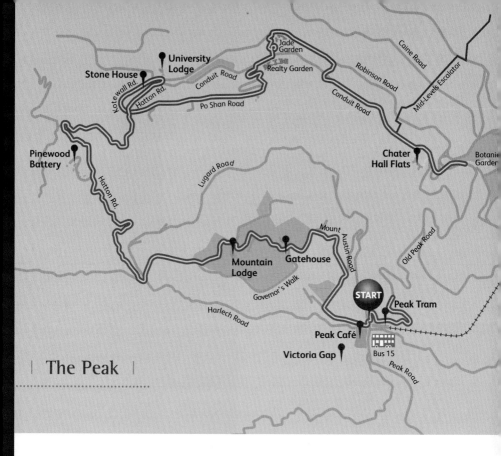

The Peak

Take the tram for a steep and quick ascent to Victoria Gap; or bus 15, for a more circuitous ride along Stubbs Road. Both deposit you near to the Peak Lookout, a long-established restaurant formerly known as the Peak Café, which was built as a rest station for sedan chair bearers. Step inside to view some old photographs.

Sedan chairs can still be seen on the Peak, but only once a year: on the occasion of the Matilda Hospital's charity race. The hospital was built in 1906 on nearby Mount Kellett by local tycoon Granville Sharp, and named after his wife. Just two years earlier, a Peak Reservation Ordinance was passed that limited residence on the Peak to those approved by the Governor. In practice, this had the effect of limiting the zone to Europeans. Sharp's will dictated that the hospital should be reserved for 'poor and helpless' patients – but only Caucasian ones. Such rules were abolished in 1946.

Renaissance gatehouse

In the days of Mountain Lodge

Traffic-free Lugard and Harlech Roads circle the Peak from the tram station, making a popular family walk with great sea views. But instead take Mount Austin Road, the middle track which leads uphill to the Peak's higher reaches. A '**mountain lodge**' was built up here in the 1860s to serve as the Governor's summer residence, away from the oppressive humidity below.

Flora Shaw, Sir Frederick Lugard's journalist wife who had been the Colonial Editor for *The Times*, waxed lyrical over the seasonal ascent. "There were still more sedan chairs and more scarlet-clad bearers to carry us up and round the sides of the rocky but flower-covered hills, through pure air which became cooler every moment," she wrote in her journal, "to find ourselves in a beautifully kept English garden with shaven lawn, tennis court and flowering shrubs and to be deposited at the foot of the steps leading up under a stone porch to a cool brown wood hall where the house servants, drawn up on either side, were awaiting their new masters."

Lady Lugard's husband didn't always share her sentiments. "It's dreadfully damp, worse than Nigeria in the rains," Sir Frederick complained after the summer of 1909, which was hotter and more humid than usual. The Peak had been wrapped in clouds for weeks on end. "Envelopes all glued together, bedsheets clammy and cigars like bits of sponge," he wrote in a familiar echo of modern complaints about the rainy season.

Stone reminder

Mountain Lodge didn't last long; typhoons ruined it and it was finally demolished in the 1940s. A new summer house was built for the Governor out at Fanling after the New Territories were acquired. The stone foundations of the original lodge survive, and have been converted into a public garden, and the **gatehouse** still stands – it's the tiny white building on your left as you go up. This was built in 1902 in Renaissance style and is now used as an office for the park gardeners.

Foundations of a once-regal residence

Mountain Lodge: pure air, pith helmets and punkah wallahs

Lord Lugard | Flora Shaw |

Pinewood Battery commanded the Western Harbour

Green ruins are now a site for picnics

The summit of Victoria Peak is occupied by radio towers and cannot be reached, but there is a good viewing point with a diagram of mountains and other harbour landmarks. Descend through the former gardens of the lodge, along what is known as **Governor's Walk**, to the small play area at the junction of Lugard and Harlech Roads. Here

Descent through the Governor's gardens

an engraved boulder commemorated the soldiers of the Middlesex Regiment who lost their lives en route to Hong Kong in 1917 when their troopship, the *Tyndareus*, struck a German mine. This boulder mysteriously disappeared one night in 1993, and after outraged letters from local heritage lovers had appeared in local newspapers, news emerged that it had been removed by members of the British armed forces in advance of their 1997 withdrawal. The stone is now housed in the National Army Museum in Chelsea, London, where a new plaque records – presumably after further investigation – that there was no loss of life on the *Tyndareus* after all.

Hatton Road leads steeply downhill to the ruins of **Pinewood Battery**. Built in 1903 on a commanding spot over the Western Harbour, its swivelling guns were intended to defend Hong Kong against encroaching French or Russian ships. As times changed in the 1920s, it was equipped with anti-aircraft artillery, but it sustained fatal damage during the Battle of Hong Kong in December 1941. The position was then manned by personnel of the 5th Regiment, Royal Artillery. On 15th December the battery was air-raided and shelled by Japanese artillery fire. One Indian gunner was killed and another wounded, while one gun was destroyed and the other badly damaged. Under these circumstances the battery was evacuated, and was never brought back into service. Today it's a popular picnic site and is a good location for sunset photography.

Cannon guards the college

Vice-Chancellor's residence

Hatton Road also has one of the surviving stones marking the 1903 boundary of the City of Victoria. Past this, the trail crosses a bridge to enter a quiet corner of the Mid-Levels. On the far side of Kotewall Road stands **University Lodge**, residence of the Vice-Chancellor. This is the upper perimeter of the University of Hong Kong's sprawling hillside campus. The attractive building dates from the 1950s, and in its garden sits an **old cannon**. This comes from the Victoria Battery which occupied this site from 1890 until its abandonment in 1914.

Turn left along Kotewall Road and take a look at No. 15, the '**Stone House**'. It's an unusual and beautifully kept mews-style building dating from 1923.

| *Mid-Levels mews* |

There's a fine **banyan** overhanging the driveway to Piccadilly Mansion. On the 18th of June 1972, a date later named 'Black Sunday', this section of **Po Shan Road** was washed downhill in a vast landslide following three days of torrential rain. The avalanche of mud smashed into a 12-storey residential tower on Kotewall Road below, which first fell backward and then collapsed, leaving 67 people dead. Incredibly, some survivors were pulled out of the rubble unharmed. Another 71 people died in similar landslides at Sau Mau Ping in Kowloon on the same day.

Generous banyan grants shade to one and all

Black Sunday: towers toppled by torrential rain

Lust, Caution –
Eileen Chang's tale
of Shanghai spies

Low-rise mansion offered a picture of the past

Further along on your right, an abandoned mansion stood empty for many years until it was demolished in 2011. This graceful three-storey building, sitting on a terrace above the road, was one of the last reminders of what much of the Mid-Levels was like until the high-rise redevelopment boom began in the 1970s. The exterior was used for establishing shots in the 2007 movie *Lust, Caution*.

As the road turns, there is a little shrine curiously dedicated to Hindu gods. Cracked steps lead down from here to a hillside garden which was frequented by Han Suyin, author of the novel *Love is a Many Splendoured Thing*, which was made into a film starring William Holden of *Suzie Wong* fame. The theme tune is still often played on local radio. The garden belonged to a mansion below – **41 Conduit Road** – which was then the premises of the Foreign Correspondents' Club, and which appeared in the film. However, the site is today occupied by Realty Gardens, and the garden is closed to non-residents.

Holden and Jones on the harbour-view verandah

The film was a hit around the world

41 Conduit Road: a palatial club for foreign correspondents

Chater's grand residence

Follow the road as it snakes downhill and turn right onto Conduit Road. This street started life in 1910 as a narrow country lane following the aqueduct which brought water from Pokfulam Reservoir to Central – hence its name. Take the steps downhill past Imperial Court. As you pass Jade Garden, you'll notice two old gateposts on either side of a driveway – as is often the case, along with foundation walls and stairways to nowhere, the only remnants of an old mansion which once stood on the site. (But look too long, and you'll be approached by a suspicious security guard who will recite the words drummed into him at guard school: "No! Private!") From here, you can walk down into Central or Sheung Wan.

Alternatively, stay on Conduit Road and continue past the Mid-Levels Escalator – an exit route down to Soho – to No. 1 Conduit Road, where a steep driveway winds up to government quarters known as **Chater Hall Flats**. Here once stood **Marble Hall**, the imposing home of venerated property tycoon Sir Catchick Paul Chater.

Chater helped establish Hong Kong Land and the Kowloon Wharf and Godown Company, and was responsible for much of the reclamation of early Central. Marble Hall, designed by local architects Leigh & Orange, was built in 1899 and stood in two acres of tropical greenery with views of the harbour.

Driveway to Marble Hall

The entrance was of fine Italian marble, as was the staircase within. Chater filled this grand residence with his collection of valuable pictures, porcelain and works of art, all of which was bequeathed to the Hong Kong Government upon his death in 1926. Marble Hall too passed to the government upon Lady Chater's death in 1935, and as Admiralty House it became home to the Naval Commander-in-Chief of the China Squadron. During the war years the great house was unfortunately damaged by fire, and afterwards stood derelict until its demolition in 1953.

From here you can follow a leafy downhill route to Central via Glenealy and the Hong Kong Zoological and Botanical Gardens.

Sir Catchick Paul Chater built a property empire

Bowen to Barker

Sir George Bowen

Named after Sir George Bowen, Irish-born governor of Hong Kong from 1883 to 1885, Bowen Road follows the level route of the Victorian aqueduct which brought water from the Tai Tam reservoirs to the city. Mostly traffic-free, shaded by a variety of trees and edged by immense granite retaining walls, it has striking views and lots of historical interest. This walk takes you from Central up to Barker Road on the Peak, via the Hong Kong Police Museum.

Cannons to cribs: the Commodore's House

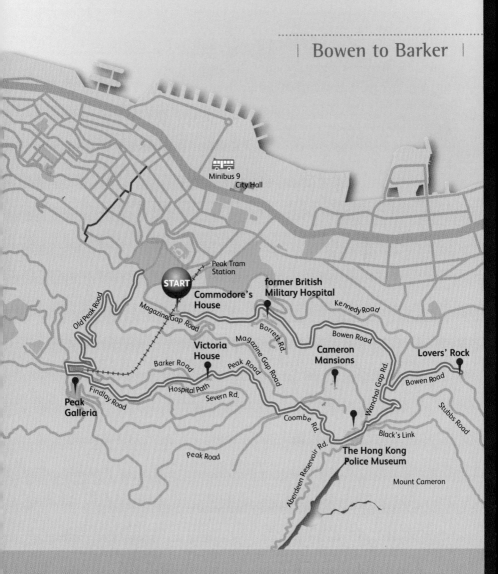

Take green minibus no. 9 from City Hall in Central or, for a bit of a climb, walk up Tramway Path which starts beside the Peak Tram station on Garden Road. The start of Bowen Road is marked by a cream-coloured colonial building occupied by Mother's Choice. Formerly known as the Commodore's House, it was used by the commanding officer of the Royal Navy until 1979.

There's a little traffic on the first section of Bowen Road as it leaves Magazine Gap Road, but not for long. At the junction with Borrett Road, a winding old track leads up to the former **British Military Hospital**, an Edwardian red-brick building which now houses kindergartens and a theatre group. Take a detour up there to inspect its attractive arched verandahs. It was built in 1903 to serve the soldiers of Victoria Barracks down the hill, and was commandeered by the Japanese for the same purpose. Despite its many owners over the years – the British Army moved out in 1967 and it then became the premises of Island School before housing various government departments – many internal features, such as floor surfaces and wooden doors, are original. During the war, the cellars were used as underground operating theatres.

Bowen Road carries on more narrowly, with views of Central and Wan Chai occasionally opening up on your left. The aqueduct which followed this route was sufficiently high above the city that few pumphouses were needed – gravity ensured good water pressure.

The road is popular with joggers. Seasonal waterfalls pour down the hillside on your right; during rain, the road is invaded by frogs. At the back of Bowen Road Garden, a rocky cascade sprays cooling water droplets into the air.

The Bowen Road aqueduct brought water to the city

War veteran: the British Military Hospital

Red-brick verandahs of the hospital

Rex Imperator: Edward VII

Fertility rites at Lovers' Rock

Soon, the steep Wanchai Gap Road crosses the trail. Also traffic-free, it runs alongside a wide stream valley which turns into a raging torrent during typhoons. A giant banyan tree is anchored beside the bridge over it. Onwards from here, you'll notice ledges where small statues and incense sticks have been placed. Finally a collection of small shrines on the left mark the steps up to **Yan Yuen Shek, or Lovers' Rock**, a standing stone visited by people, mainly women, seeking marriage or children. It's painted partly red and adorned with banners, rosettes and incense. The phallic rock has probably been venerated in this way for thousands of years, long before any permanent settlement appeared around the harbour below.

Below the monolith, another shrine of red-inked rocks also receives a steady stream of visitors. A local legend tells of a Hong Kong girl who had a wartime affair with a Japanese soldier, and the two would meet secretly at Lovers' Rock. When the war ended, the soldier had to return to Japan, and the girl decided to take her own life. There may be more to this tale than meets the eye.

Backtrack now to Wanchai Gap Road and follow it uphill to emerge at Wanchai Gap itself. This pass is a meeting point for seven mountain roads. Second on your left, the pedestrian Black's Link rises up the sides of Mount Cameron; a good walk for another day, it was built by Major-General W. Black to allow military access to the Peak. This was an unpopular move with polite Peak society, since it allowed the army to billet soldiers in the Peak Hotel and lower the tone of the exclusive area.

The Hong Kong Police Museum is clearly signposted away to the right. A cannon once belonging to the East India Company guards the steps up to the building, which was originally a police station itself but has housed the police memorabilia collection since 1988. Inside you'll find exhibitions on triad societies, narcotics, insignia, changing uniforms, weaponry and other historical aspects of local law enforcement.

The Hong Kong Police Force was founded by Major William Caine in the early 1840s, with a small band of military men as its first recruits. Hong Kong was a lawless, buccaneering place then, and the force had to develop quickly to bring order to a city which attracted all the vagabonds and criminals of the China coast. It became a multi-ethnic constabulary of Chinese, Indian and European extraction. The force was awarded the prefix 'Royal' in recognition of its steadfastness during the Communist-inspired riots of 1967. Today, it's one of the largest police forces in the world, comparable in size to those of London and New York.

Set up so soon after the founding of Hong Kong, the police force's history mirrors that of the city.

Commanding position – the Police Museum on the Peak

Pipe dreams: millions of people became addicted to opium

Somniferous smoke

Cash crop – fortunes were made from the poppy

One exhibition gallery covers the opium trade. Hong Kong owes its modern existence to the sale of Indian opium to China; it was this lucrative trade, and the restrictions placed by Canton officials upon it, which prompted the Opium Wars. It seems that opium was the opium of the people in those days – China in particular had an inexhaustible thirst for the potent poppy, and Western merchants were only too happy to supply it. The social effects were disastrous: over a quarter of the male Chinese population became addicts. By 1909, international pressure forced a ban on the import of the drug to China. But by that stage, a large portion of Hong Kong's population was addicted to opium's sweet dreams, and the government was equally addicted to the huge tax revenues it brought in. It was only after 1945 that the drug was officially banned locally.

The Hong Kong Police Force is unusual in that it has held responsibilities far beyond normal policing; handling immigration and customs duties until the 1960s, and even guarding the border with China today. To deal with this task, and events like the influx of Vietnamese boat people in the 1970s, it maintains paramilitary capabilities and a large marine division. The post-war Commissioner of Police, Duncan MacIntosh, built a chain of fortified observation

posts along the border in the early 1950s; this followed a series of incidents in 1949 in which policemen were ambushed by bandits – or defeated Kuomintang soldiers – from the Chinese side. Known as MacIntosh Cathedrals for their distinctive shape, they are still in place along the Shenzhen River today, and are listed as historic buildings.

The police museum is open every day except Mondays.

Opium-smoking paraphernalia

A samurai sword may be buried beneath Cameron Mansions

Return to Coombe Road, a quiet, tree-lined lane, and turn right. At the crossroads, you can take a detour up the higher end of Magazine Gap Road to reach **Cameron Mansions**. These apartments stand on massive retaining walls which are out of all proportion to the modest buildings above them. These are in fact the surviving foundations of the **Japanese War Memorial**, a huge project which was commenced, but never finished, in 1942.

Plans called for a 40-metre tower to stand on top of a granite-clad earthen platform. As well as a monument to the Japanese soldiers who had sacrificed their lives in the conquest of Hong Kong, the structure was intended to function as a Shinto shrine, along the lines of the Yasukuni Shrine in Tokyo. But it may have been more than this: in the post-war trials, Major Hirao Yoshio suggested it was designed as a place for all Japanese to gather and commit ritual suicide in the event of Britain retaking Hong Kong by force. In the event, Japan's sudden surrender in 1945 meant that no such battle was necessary.

Work began, using Chinese labourers to carry stone up the hill to the construction site, and a Shinto priest conducted a blessing ceremony in which a centuries-old samurai sword was placed in a box and buried under the flight of stairs ascending the platform. It may still be there, somewhere beneath the modern apartments.

When Admiral Harcourt's British fleet sailed victorious into the harbour in August 1945 (following spread), the half-completed monument was starkly visible on the denuded skyline of Hong Kong Island. As a symbol of occupation and wartime suffering, it could not remain. "The huge monolithic concrete Japanese war memorial on the Peak was greatly resented by locals and service people alike," recalled Lieutenant Jack Button, who sailed in on HMS *Indomitable*. "I took a photograph of it and shortly after our visit the Royal Engineers blew it up." Demolition wasn't an easy task, however; the twelve-legged tower was made of reinforced concrete and must have weighed several hundred tons, and it took months to prepare it for dynamiting. On the day of destruction, crowds gathered along Magazine Gap Road to watch the remains of the tower fall. "When the smoke cleared, the ruin of Japan's mute symbol of attempted domination was revealed to the cheering crowd," reported the *South China Morning Post* at the time. The foundations were left intact, and Cameron Mansions later built upon them.

No. 33 Magazine Gap Road, the tall white building opposite, is one of the few pre-war buildings left on the Peak. It was probably built in the 1920s and is used as staff quarters by HSBC.

Back at the crossroads, follow Peak Road uphill and turn immediately right onto Barker Road. It's another peaceful hillside route with little traffic. The first item of interest is **Victoria House** at No. 15: the residence of the Chief Secretary for Administration, the second-in-command in the Hong Kong Government. The post was known as Colonial Secretary until 1976. As with Government House, official banquets are thrown here every year.

Shinto shrine: the War Memorial

The Japanese War Memorial was clearly seen from the deck of Harcourt's flagship

Former maternity
block, now
government quarters

Hospital staff
gather around the
foundation stone

The jubilee stone
is still in place
today

High office: residence of the Chief Secretary

The two-storey residence sits on the former site of the **Victoria Hospital for Women and Children**, and the foundation stone of this building can be found beside a thriving banyan tree a little further on. It's dated the 22nd of June 1897, the day of Queen Victoria's Diamond Jubilee, when she celebrated sixty years on the throne. Governor Sir William Robinson put his name to the stone, along with another on Victoria Road in Pokfulam the same day; his sedan chair bearers must have earned their money on that summer afternoon.

The building directly behind the stone is the maternity block of the old hospital, and this dates from 1921 although it looks newer. The hospital closed in 1947. The old maternity block, renamed Victoria Flats, is now used as government staff quarters.

Follow in the footsteps of Victorian porters by climbing Hospital Path, which leads onto the narrow lanes of Severn Road and then Findlay Road – named for Alexander Findlay Smith, the man who built the Peak Tram. The Lions Pavilion, always busy with tourists photographing the view, heralds your arrival at the tram's upper terminus.

The Peak Galleria, on your left, occupies the site of the old **Peak Hotel**. Opened by Dorabjee Naorojee, the Parsee entrepreneur, it didn't meet the same success as his Star Ferry operations: the Peak's misty climate discouraged visitors, damp set in, it was bought out by the rival Hongkong Hotel, and it finally burnt down in 1938.

On the plaza, the Hong Kong Tourism Board has opened an information centre inside a 1950s-vintage tram car. You can return to town by tram, bus, minibus, or – if your knees are up to the steep descent – by following Old Peak Road downhill to Central.

Despite its location beside the tram terminus, the Peak Hotel failed to attract business

Mid-Levels view of a low-rise Central in the 1950s

Hong Kong University and Sai Ying Pun

The University of Hong Kong, the territory's first such institution, often appears in lists of the world's top universities. It has come a long way in its short history – only inaugurated in 1912, it has yet to celebrate its centenary. This route starts off in the university grounds and then takes you through Sai Ying Pun, an old district with plenty of historical interest.

At the end of the 19th century, Western-style universities were being founded across China, but these were generally operated by missionary societies with an explicitly Christian ethic. The Hong Kong business community favoured the establishment of a more secular institution, similar to those in Britain, and the idea received wide support. A Hong Kong College of Medicine had existed since 1887 – training, among others, Dr Sun Yat-sen, the man later to found the Republic of China – and it was decided to use this well regarded school as the nucleus of a new university.

The Governor of the day, Sir Frederick Lugard, provided land on the hillside at Pokfulam, and a fund-raising drive commenced. Lugard's wife, the famous journalist Flora Shaw, assisted. Only £300 was forthcoming from the Colonial Office in London, so the bulk of cash had to come from local sources. The Viceroy of Canton contributed funds, as did Hormusjee Mody, a generous Parsee businessman, and the foundation stone was laid in 1910. The first intake consisted of 200 students, a far cry from today's student total of nearly 24,000. Ten years after the founding, women students were admitted for the first time.

| Viceroy Yuan Shu-hsun | Sir Frederick Lugard | Hormusjee Mody |

Looted for firewood: after the war, a big repair job

Queen's Road West

First Street

Second Street

Third Street

High Street

Centre for Heritage

Third Street

Kau Yan Church

King's College

Hing Hon Road

Yu Lok Lane

Western Street

Centre Street

Eastern Street

Queen's Road

Hospital Road

King George V Memorial Park

Edwardian building

Old Lunatic Asylum

Bonham Road

START

Pokfulam Road

Loke Yew Hall

Bonham Road

Fung Ping Shan Museum

Babington Path

Lyttelton Road

Library Building

The University of Hong Kong

Eliot Hall

May Hall

University Drive

Kotewall Road

Hong Kong University and Sai Ying Pun

Cat Street

Upper Lascar Row

Blake Garden

Po Hing Fong

ood Road

Man Mo Temple

Hong Kong Museum of Medical Sciences

Lugard left quite a legacy in Hong Kong. Besides the university, he oversaw the construction of the Kowloon-Canton Railway, another major project which required Chinese cooperation. But his posting as Governor was but a brief interlude in a career of African empire-building. He described his duties here as comparatively restful – suffering fools gladly and signing documents incessantly – but this may have been a little modest; he also had to deal with the unrest surrounding the fall of the Qing dynasty in 1911. Outside Hong Kong, he is best known for the creation of Nigeria.

This walk starts at the West Gate, on Pokfulam Road, reachable by bus from Central. Turn left upon entering the compound to reach **Loke Yew Hall**, a graceful Renaissance-style building which has become a symbol of the university as a whole. It's named after an Overseas Chinese benefactor who operated tin mines in Malaya. Opposite, the domed Hung Hing Ying Building was built in 1919 to serve as the students' union. The university was badly looted during the Second World War – even roof beams were removed, probably for firewood.

Loke Yew's legacy – the university's main building

Father of the nation: Sun Yat-sen

May Hall was built as student accommodation

A bronze bust of the knighted Mody can be found on the main staircase of Loke Yew Hall, and you can walk up and through the building, via courtyards of impressively tall palm trees, to reach the main library behind. As they are built over a sprawling hillside estate, the campus buildings are connected at various levels by covered walkways, lifts and escalators.

Sir Loke Yew

Sun Yat-sen Steps lead up to the university bookshop. A foundation stone on the steps marks the regeneration programme started in 1978. Bearing left past the lily pond garden takes you through the university cafeteria – a decent place to stop for a cheap lunch – and then up to a plaza in front of **Eliot Hall** and **May Hall**. These red-brick student hostels were built in 1914 and 1915, and were pressed into service as emergency hospitals during the Japanese invasion in 1941. Their eastern wings collapsed in a landslide brought on by Typhoon Wanda in 1962, which killed 130 people in its destructive passage over Hong Kong.

Cloistered courtyard

A third building in identical style, Lugard Hall, formerly stood in front of them but was demolished in 1992. Above them, steps lead up past some great banyans to University Lodge and the cannon mentioned (see page 18), but it is difficult to view. You can however use this route as an exit to Kotewall Road.

From the plaza in front of Eliot Hall, take the steps down and to the left to pass through the K. K. Leung Building. Lifts travel down to the East Gate on Bonham Road, where you can step inside the **Fung Ping Shan Museum**,

Open space on the university campus

built in 1932. Originally used as a library housing the university's Chinese book collection, and then as offices for the Hong Kong University Press, it's now a gallery of Chinese artworks. Perhaps its most notable asset is the world's largest collection of Yuan-dynasty Nestorian crosses.

Sir Samuel Bonham

Bonham Road recalls **Sir Samuel Bonham**, Governor of Hong Kong from 1848 to 1854, who was popular partly because Sir John Davis, his predecessor, was so reviled. Bonham had previously been Governor of the Straits Settlements (Singapore, Penang and Malacca) and brought regional experience to the job. Hong Kong was still a new and unproven addition to Queen Victoria's growing empire; the little port was crime-ridden, disease-infested and insolvent. Under Bonham's calm guidance, the colony moved towards success in trade – American whaling ships began calling in for supplies, and Hong Kong became the embarkation point for the droves of mainland Chinese emigrating to find their fortunes overseas. Bonham Strand on the former waterfront in Sheung Wan is also named after Sir Samuel.

It's worth making a brief detour down Hing Hon Road to see the old back-street residential buildings at Nos. 2 and 19, which date from around 1916 – rare sights in today's Hong Kong. These Western-influenced types of tenement houses were built by Chinese as they became more affluent and moved uphill into the Mid-Levels. Hing Hon is a private road, a rarity in itself, and the stairs used as a short cut by students are gated off in the evenings.

Returning to Bonham Road and turning left, an ornamental archway leads up to the **Tang Chi Ngong Building**, now the university's Centre of Asian Studies, which was opened as the School of Chinese in 1931. Opposite, **King's College** has occupied the top corner of Western Street since 1926. It's a government school which has occasionally been turned over to other purposes: in 1927 it was commandeered by the British Shanghai Defence Force, en route to its mission to reinforce the International Settlement's garrison, and during the later war years it was used by Japanese forces as a stable. Look over the wall to see its front courtyard and fountain.

Fount of learning: King's College

Further down Western Street – past the very Gothic-style **Kau Yan Church**, dating from 1932 – the Western District Community Centre occupies the original building of the Tsan Yuk Hospital. It was built in 1922 as the first maternity hospital for Chinese mothers and played an important role in reducing infant mortality. It's now home to various local organizations, including the Sai Ying Pun *kaifong* (neighbourhood welfare committee). You can go inside to see original features like the graceful curved staircase. Below the hospital, there's a public bathhouse, a survivor of the days when most households lacked running water.

Gothic survivor – Kau Yan Church

Old staff quarters: the Centre for Heritage

Graceful sweep of the hospital staircase

The old staff quarters behind the hospital, a lovely little building hidden behind a tree, is now the **Conservancy Association's Centre for Heritage**, which holds regular exhibitions. The Association has been advocating local heritage protection for much longer than it has been fashionable, first campaigning for sustainable development as far back as 1968.

From the other side of Third Street, take the steps up between the yellow shops to find **Yu Lok Lane**, a hidden neighbourhood of small 1940s buildings. The street is to be demolished by the Urban Renewal Authority and replaced by the usual high-rise development, probably faced with cheap bathroom tiles like the new building on the other side of Centre Street. The old houses are in terrible condition and few will mourn their passing, but other cities such as Macau see value in preserving their old neighbourhoods instead of neglecting and then destroying them.

Gated community – but not for much longer

Turn right onto Centre Street, a steep incline of markets which has a view straight down to the harbour, and cross High Street. This part of Sai Ying Pun is an orderly grid of streets named after directions and numbers. High Street should logically be Fourth Street, but due to its pronunciation in Cantonese sounding too similar to the word for death, the number four is not popular locally.

Back on Bonham Road, the Czarina Restaurant stands immediately on your right. It's been serving Pirozhki and Beef Stroganoff, among local dishes, since 1964. The 'White' (i.e. anti-Bolshevik) Russians in Hong Kong were émigrés who had to flee Communist takeovers not once but twice: from Russia after the October Revolution of 1917, and then from Shanghai, Harbin and other parts of China after 1949. Present in large numbers in the 1950s before emigrating further afield, they opened restaurants and bakeries – Queen's Café and Cherikoff being the most famous – and introduced borsch to local menus, where it strangely remains.

Next door to it, **No. 35 Bonham Road** is an elegant **Edwardian** survivor. Partly concealed by giant hoardings of popular 'pseudo-model' Chrissie Chau, you can only appreciate its proportions – not those of the model – by crossing the road.

Its design is a legacy of stringent regulations introduced in 1903 to govern the dimensions of Hong Kong's residential buildings. The objective was to avoid the outbreaks of plague and other diseases that had flourished in the previous century. New buildings would be no higher than four storeys, and depths of more than 12 metres were allowed only if every floor was provided with windows for adequate lighting and ventilation. Within these rules, domestic buildings with deep, colonnaded balconies began to replace the previous cluttered tenements. Strong bonds of attachment were formed between these graceful new houses and those fortunate enough to occupy them; bonds that in some cases have lasted generations and ensured the survival of beloved homes such as this one.

Hanging gardens of pot plants help preserve the illusion that all is as it was in the outside world.

*Edwardian elegance:
deep balconies made
the most of air and light*

Carry on east along Bonham Road and take the steps downhill just past the bus stop. The **Old Lunatic Asylum** – presumably open to lunatics of all ages, despite its present name – was built in 1891 to house Chinese psychiatric patients. It's a small two-storey building only designed to keep up to 20 people, since most inmates were sent back to China for treatment. It's now used as a methadone clinic. The colonnaded red-brick building is in good condition and its courtyard has a nice crop of palm trees.

The arched asylum now caters to recovering heroin addicts

Opposite stands the Old Mental Hospital, or at least its surviving stone façade, which has been incorporated into the new community complex behind it. This impressive granite edifice was built in 1892 as somewhat oversized accommodation for ten European nurses. It was occupied by the Japanese military police during the war, converted into a female psychiatric hospital afterwards, and then in 1971 was abandoned and essentially left to rot for nearly 30 years. The dark, rather forbidding building, associated with war and mental illness, was visited only by vagrants, teenage ghost hunters and heroin addicts from the methadone centre next door, and it gained a reputation as a haunted house. Two fires damaged much of the interior, and the roof collapsed. Finally most of the structure behind the façade was demolished – the chimneys finding new homes atop Murray House in Stanley, and some bricks going to repair the battery at the Museum of Coastal Defence – and the new centre was opened in 2001.

A venerable banyan overhangs the corner entrance into **King George V Memorial Park**. Laid out in the 1930s, after the death of the king, its creation was part of a policy to bring breathing space into crowded tenement areas. It occupies the grounds of the former Government Civil Hospital – hence the immense granite retaining walls, old balustrades and grand north entrance.

Spooky Hall: the Old Mental Hospital

Standing beside the football pitch and looking back at the Old Mental Hospital, you can see a more modernist building with large balconies overlooking the park from the left. This is the old Upper Levels Police Station, built in 1935 and used until 2005 as offices for the regional Crime Wing. Its style, a hybrid of Art Deco and Stripped Classicism, makes great use of symmetry. It's currently being renovated to serve as the new home of the David Trench Rehabilitation Centre, which is moving from Bonham Road to make way for the new Sai Ying Pun MTR station.

The modern Tsan Yuk Hospital, built in 1955 to replace the original one visited earlier, faces the north entrance of the park. Turn right and follow Hospital Road uphill, past old ornamental railings, and take the steps down Pound Lane, named for the government animal pound which once existed here. It's hard to imagine now, but people once kept cows and goats in the urban areas and let them graze on the hillsides above the city.

Blake Garden is another green space which was created expressly to improve public health. It was here, in the notoriously overcrowded and unsanitary Tai Ping Shan district, that a major outbreak of bubonic plague occurred in 1894. At its height, the epidemic was causing 100 deaths a day. Troops of the Shropshire Light Infantry were brought in to cleanse everything with quicklime, a disinfectant, and to remove corpses for mass burial in ditches; but suspicious inhabitants smuggled the bodies of the dead and dying from house to house to avoid such an indignity. In an effort to eradicate the plague, the government offered two cents for every dead rat handed in, but after 45,000 rodents were produced, the rewards had to be cancelled. Eventually the worst slum area was razed to the ground, requiring the eviction of 7,000 people, and this garden was laid out in its place. It's named after Governor Sir Henry Blake, instigator of the rat hunt.

Shibasaburo Kitasato   *Alexandre Yersin*

Plague prevention: the Old Pathological Institute

At the time, the specific cause of plague was still unknown, but this mystery was solved almost simultaneously by two scientists working at the heart of the epidemic. **Shibasaburo Kitasato** of Japan and **Alexandre Yersin** of Switzerland both discovered and isolated the *Yersinia pestis* plague bacillus. Up a flight of steps from Blake Garden, the Old Pathological Institute commemorates their achievement, since it is now the **Hong Kong Museum of Medical Sciences**. The museum, an elegant Edwardian building of brickwork and arched verandahs, is run by a private society. Inside there are exhibitions on local medical history – including recent events such as SARS – while outside a herb garden displays some of the basic ingredients of both Western and Chinese medicine.

Follow any street downhill from here; they all cross Hollywood Road to reach **Cat Street**, officially known as Upper Lascar Row. 'Lascar' is an archaic word once used to describe seamen from India and Southeast Asia, who would have come ashore and stayed in this area in the 19th century. *Mor lor* – which appears in the Chinese name of the street, as well as in Mosque Street – means the same, though with negative connotations. It was only in 2009 that suggestions arose to rename these streets, to avoid causing offence in these more sensitive times. Probably the best course of action is for the affected community to reclaim the word themselves; it's hard to offend Western residents with the term *gwailo*, for instance, as it has been defused by common usage.

Cat Street is lined with stalls and shops selling all sorts of antiques, old photographs, obsolete coinage, Mao badges, advertising posters and other curios, and you can enjoy browsing even though authenticity may not always be guaranteed.

Bric-a-brac: junk and gems alike are recycled on Cat Street

Pok Fu Lam

The green western slopes of Hong Kong Island have long been used as a retreat from the city – first by missionaries and dairy farmers, and today by students and wealthier residents. Starting at the Peak and ending atop Mount Davis, this walk will exercise your knees and give you advance views of the heritage sites along the way.

Victoria Gap, where the Peak Tower stands, is a crossroads from which trails lead in half a dozen directions. The entrance to Pok Fu Lam Country Park is easily found directly opposite the bus station, and a car-free road leads straight down into peaceful forest. Old banyans clinging to the stone walls shade your descent into the valley.

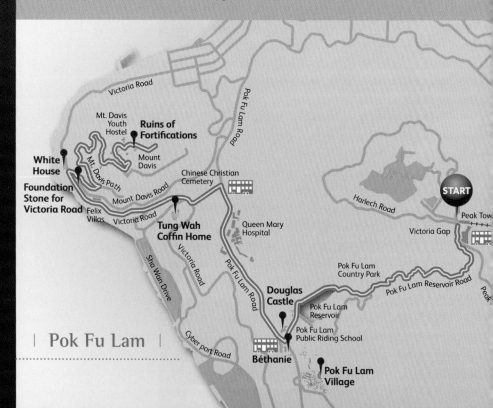

Pok Fu Lam

Roots of aged
banyans spread
as far as their
branches

*Spring rains flow to fill
the reservoir below*

These steep hillsides were saved from development by the need to protect Hong Kong's water sources. This valley was dammed as early as 1863 and a reservoir – **the colony's first** – was built down below to supply water to the city. An aqueduct ran around from Pok Fu Lam to Central, giving Conduit Road its name. Major tree planting took place at the same time to prevent soil erosion. Before then, most of Hong Kong Island's uplands were bare, partly thanks to the grass cutters who scoured the hills to collect kindling. The forest suffered during the war years, when much of it was chopped down for firewood; but it has recovered well and you're now able to walk through mature woodland.

Camellia and eagle's claw flowers provide colour beside the path, and birdsong fills the air. In fact, it was the 'pok fu' bird which gave Pok Fu Lam its name – *lam* meaning 'forest' – although the original Chinese characters have changed. It's often pronounced 'Pock Fulham' by expats more familiar with the London football club.

At the only fork in the road, turn right to carry on downhill, passing some **bricked-up bunkers** built by the British Army. The path now skirts the reservoir. Beside the dam, there's an attractive old building now used by the country parks staff, and facing it an information board with old photos of the area. One picture shows a strange white castle which seems very out of place on the bare hillside. In fact this building is still there:

Witnesses of warfare

now known as University Hall, it's hidden from view by trees. As you pass the riding school on your left, the mansion stands above the other side of the road. You can go up the steps and through the low gateway for a closer look.

Pokfulam of the past, a world away from worry

Today, greener hillsides and busier waters

Gothic palace for a Scots taipan, now students' quarters

Douglas Castle, as it was originally called, was built in the 1860s by Scottish taipan Douglas Lapraik to serve as his country home. It looked rather different then: an octagonal penthouse surrounded by battlements commanded all-round sea views, four crenellated corner towers had mock arrow slits, and outhouses were built in identical Victorian Gothic style. The building has undergone many changes over the years and is now used as halls of residence for Hong Kong University students.

Lapraik arrived on the China coast as a young man, travelling to Macau in 1839 to become apprentice to an English watchmaker. Upon the founding of Hong Kong a few years later, he moved to the new colony and quickly became successful in the property and shipping trades. He built a dock at Aberdeen to service Royal Navy vessels, ran a line of steamships up the coast to Amoy and Foochow (modern Xiamen and Fuzhou) and helped establish the Hong Kong Chamber of Commerce. He was one of the investors in the Chinese junk *Keying* which made history by sailing to London and New York in 1846 – the boat amazed the crowds there, including Queen Victoria, who

Douglas Lapraik, early entrepreneur

had never seen such a thing before. Perhaps his most notable legacy was the founding in 1863 of the Hongkong & Whampoa Dock Company (see page 313). This was the first limited company in Hong Kong – prompting the government to start writing a Companies Ordinance – and its ultimate successor, Cheung Kong, still bears stock code 0001 at the Hong Kong Stock Exchange. The Douglas Steamship Company remained in existence until the 1980s.

After an outstanding career, Lapraik retired to Britain, and Douglas Castle was sold to the French Mission in 1894. The priests renamed it Nazareth House, added a chapel, and installed a printing press which produced religious texts in dozens of Asian languages. A prominent feature added at this time was the cast-iron spiral staircase which connects three floors. In 1954 the building passed into its current ownership; the chapel was converted into a dining hall and the crypt into a common room, and as University Hall it continues to house undergraduate students. Despite the building's change of name, alumni are known as Castlers.

Béthanie stands on the other side of Pok Fu Lam Road. Built in 1873 by the same French Mission, it was designed as a peaceful retreat and sanatorium for priests returning from missionary work in China and elsewhere in the Far East. The *Missions Etrangères de Paris* departed in the 1970s, and for many years the building deteriorated while being used as a storehouse by Hong Kong University Press. Since 2003 it has been occupied by the Hong Kong Academy for Performing Arts, who have renovated it in innovative style: in particular, the original pitched roof, which was removed at some point in the past, has been reinstated using glass panels instead of tiles. The project won the UNESCO Asia-Pacific Heritage Award in 2008.

There's a French Mission museum in the former wine cellar which is open every day until 6:00 pm, and guided tours of the building are also conducted. The *Bauhinia blakeana*, Hong Kong's official floral emblem, was discovered growing in the gardens of Béthanie by French priests in the 1880s.

On the far side of the building, two octagonal cowsheds have survived from the earliest days of Hong Kong's milk industry – they gave rise to the company which became Dairy Farm.

Wedding services take place in the chapel at Béthanie

Peaceful retreat for the French fathers

It was a Scottish pioneer of tropical medicine, Dr Patrick Manson, who came up with the idea of establishing a farm to supply hygienic fresh milk to the European population of Hong Kong. Eighty cows were imported and the **Dairy Farm** company began operations in 1886. The company later diversified into running supermarkets, in a joint venture with the Lane Crawford department store, until it bought the Wellcome retail chain and became part of the Jardines group.

The Pok Fu Lam farm was closed in 1983, and the two cattle sheds have now been converted into a **performance space** – one as a tiny theatre and the other as a foyer, which also has a small photo exhibition of the site's history. Down the hill from these, another of the old Dairy Farm buildings is now used by the Chinese Cuisine Training Institute.

Across the road, **Pok Fu Lam Village** may look like a shanty town but it is in fact one of the few indigenous settlements remaining on Hong Kong Island. A lot of villagers were formerly employed on the dairy farm. Today, some of them grow crops on land which must be worth billions. Besides a large earth god shrine, the village has an unusual brick tower called the **Lee Ling Immortal Pagoda** which dates from about 1910.

Take a bus now a few stops north, passing the Queen Mary Hospital, to alight at the **Chinese Christian Cemetery**. The site has excellent *feng shui*, with wooded hills behind it and an unencumbered view out to sea. A stairway leads straight down through the terraces to the Pavilion of Eternity – 'Erected by Wing Lock Tong, May 1951' – and then to Victoria Road. Bear right and then take the steps down into a ramshackle stonemasons' village. At the foot of the hill you'll find the gates to the **Tung Wah Coffin Home**, a complex of buildings reminiscent of old Macau.

| *In transit: traditional coffins* |

VICTORIA ROAD

THIS STONE WAS LAID BY

SIR WILLIAM ROBINSON K. C. M. G.

GOVERNOR

TO COMMEMORATE THE COMPLETION OF THE 60TH YEAR OF THE REIGN OF

HER MOST GRACIOUS MAJESTY

QUEEN VICTORIA

Jubilee monument to the Empress of India

From the late 19th century onwards, tens of thousands of mainland Chinese people passed through Hong Kong on their way to Southeast Asia, North America, Australia and other places where fortunes in tin, gold or plain labour could be made. When they died, their wish was to be buried in their ancestral lands, and so their bodies were sent back the way they came. There was a need for temporary storage of their remains until transport could be found back to China, particularly in times of strife on the mainland, and so the trustees of the Man Mo temple on Hollywood Road founded the first coffin home in Kennedy Town in 1875. This was moved to the present site in 1899, and the Tung Wah Hospital took over its management. It is still in use; good burial plots can be hard to find in crowded Hong Kong, and caskets and urns can be kept here until one becomes available.

The site was nicely restored in 2004, winning praise from the Hong Kong Heritage Awards, but it's private and you may not be allowed into the compound.

Further west along Victoria Road, Felix Villas is an elegant terrace of houses built in the 1920s and now used as quarters for university staff. Beyond it, a foundation stone for Victoria Road is set into its junction with Mount Davis Road. This was laid in 1897 to mark Queen Victoria's 60th year on the throne; construction of the road commenced at the same time and was named in her honour. It was moved to its present site in 1977, coincidentally also a royal jubilee year, and a plate notes this fact.

Victoria's secret: the prison with no name

On the coastal side of the road further on from here, **a compound of white buildings** behind a high wall has no sign, nor any official name on maps; not even a street number. Since the handover in 1997, it has been slowly crumbling into the surrounding greenery. Originally the mess of the Royal Engineers, the compound was transferred to the police force in the 1950s for use as a secret prison for Taiwanese spies – the colonial government was keen to avoid Hong Kong being used as a proxy battleground for Chinese Nationalist and Communist forces, and Special Branch detained anyone suspected of engaging in espionage.

But it was in 1967 that things really heated up. That summer, Hong Kong was rocked by riots inspired by the chaos of the Cultural Revolution over the border. Home-made bombs were planted in the streets. Leftists called strikes which paralysed public transport. Unionist demonstrators clashed with police,

pro-Beijing crowds waving Mao's red book picketed Government House, and a radio journalist who opposed the violence was murdered. At the border town of Sha Tau Kok, Chinese militia shot and killed a group of Hong Kong police officers. Fearing a possible invasion, the government decided to take radical action: pro-communist schools and newspapers were closed down, and the police were granted special powers to arrest leftist leaders. This involved the world's first helicopter raids on multi-storey buildings. The political prisoners were brought to Pok Fu Lam and held in solitary confinement until the disturbances were over.

This hard-line response was generally supported by the Hong Kong public – the leftists' violence having turned public opinion against them – and in appreciation of its steadfastness, the Hong Kong Police Force was later given the prefix 'Royal', which it kept until 1997. In Macau, by contrast, the

Portuguese authorities failed to maintain order during the unrest, and control of the enclave was effectively handed over to China thirty years early.

The '**white house**' compound may last have been used in 1989, when democratic activists smuggled away from the massacre in Tiananmen Square were debriefed here before being sent abroad. The Beijing crackdown prompted Hong Kong people of all political stripes to assist an emergency 'underground railroad' operation. Led by the Hong Kong Alliance in Support of Patriotic Democratic Movements in China, which still organizes the annual commemoration in Victoria Park, Operation Yellow Bird helped hundreds of students and intellectuals escape from the mainland. One such person involved was Lo Hoi-sing; formerly Hong Kong's top man in China as head of the Trade Development Council's Beijing office, his involvement in the rescue missions landed him in a mainland jail, and his career never recovered. Most of the details of the risky operation remain a secret.

Special Branch was disbanded as 1997 approached – some local detectives were given British passports to protect them from any post-handover retaliation – and the buildings have been empty since then.

| Prison gates | Officers' quarters left to ruin |

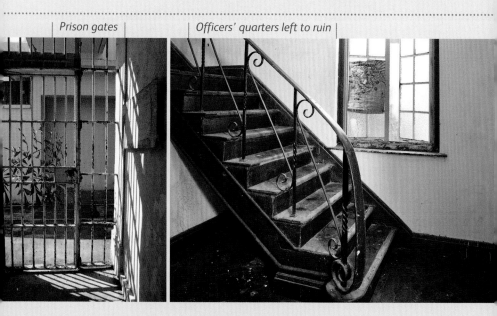

Winds of change have allowed nature to reclaim the compound

Approaching the fort

The final stretch of this route involves a hike up quiet Mount Davis Path. A flight of 365 steps leads up to an isolated youth hostel, from which backpackers can enjoy 270-degree views of Victoria Harbour. To save their legs, a shuttle bus service links it to Sheung Wan.

Past the hostel, and up a steep slope built to haul giant 9.2-inch guns to the summit of this coastal peak, you'll find the ruins of an extensive system of fortifications. Mount Davis is well positioned to guard the western approaches to the harbour, and five gun emplacements were built here in the early years of the 20th century to ward off potential French or Russian fleets. More cannons were installed at Jubilee Battery, at the foot of the peak. They were of little use against a land-based army, however, so were unable to defend Hong Kong during the Japanese invasion from the mainland in 1941. They came under heavy aircraft attack during the assault – and the damage can still be seen – but the last defenders held out right until the surrender on Christmas Day.

As well as exploring the bunkers, tunnels and command posts, you can end your walk the same way it was started: with panoramic views of sea and islands.

Remains of the gun emplacements

Troops man the Mount Davis battery

The position took direct hits during 1941

Today, hikers can explore the fort's trenches

Heavy cannons hauled by rope up the hillside

Sheung Wan and Hollywood Road

The urban districts directly west of Central were the first to be laid out after the British took possession of Hong Kong. They were settled mostly by Chinese, since the colonial elite of the time preferred to live higher up the hill. Follow this easy route through Sheung Wan and back to Central to discover something of Hong Kong's 19th-century past.

From Central, take any tram west along Des Voeux Road to the Edwardian-era **Western Market**. Hemmed in now by an elevated highway, it stood on the waterfront when it was built in 1906. It closed as a poultry and fish market in the 1980s and underwent restoration to reopen as a specialist shopping mall.

Bandaged brickwork, built to last

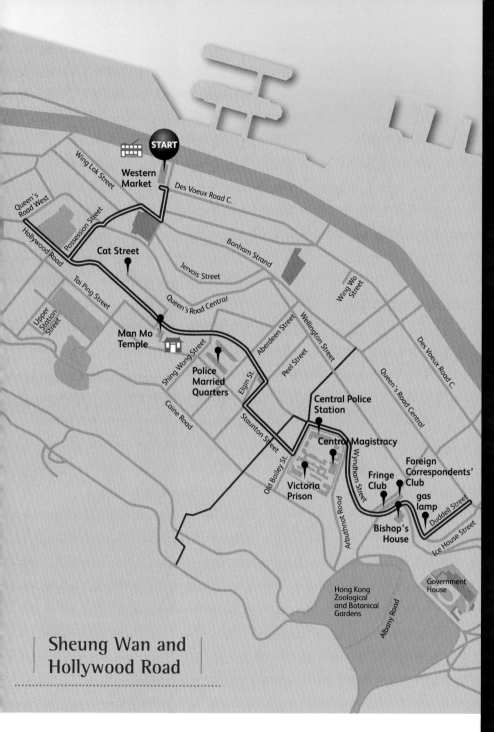

START

Western Market

Wing Lok Street

Des Voeux Road C.

Queen's Road West

Hollywood Road

Possession Street

Bonham Strand

Cat Street

Jervois Street

Tai Ping Street

Queen's Road Central

Wing Wo Street

Upper Station Street

Man Mo Temple

Shing Wong Street

Police Married Quarters

Aberdeen Street

Wellington Street

Peel Street

Des Voeux Road C.

Caine Road

Elgin St.

Queen's Road Central

Staunton Street

Central Police Station

Central Magistracy

Old Bailey St.

Victoria Prison

Wyndham Street

Fringe Club

Foreign Correspondents' Club

gas lamp

Duddell Street

Arbuthnot Road

Bishop's House

Ice House Street

Hong Kong Zoological and Botanical Gardens

Albany Road

Government House

Sheung Wan and Hollywood Road

The restaurant on the second floor serves dim sum and holds dance classes, its atmosphere greatly enhanced by the original brickwork and iron roof braces. The cloth merchants on the first floor were relocated from Wing On Street, one of the busy alleyways which formerly existed on the site of Grand Millennium Plaza.

Letter-writing for amahs, a vanished trade

The older north block of the market wasn't lucky enough to be preserved: its site is now occupied by the giant Sheung Wan municipal complex.

The warren of streets between Des Voeux Road and Queen's Road at this point – **Bonham Strand**, Wing Lok Street and Jervois Street – were very early established as the home of Chinese trading houses or 'hongs' which traded goods between Southeast Asia and China. In fact the area was known as *Nam Pak Hong* – 'North-South Company' – after the tradesmen's union. Jervois Street's Chinese name, *So Hong Gai*, refers to Suzhou and Hangzhou, two ports on the China coast. You can still find shops selling all manner of items imported from Southeast Asia, including rice, bird's nest, dried seafood and traditional medicines. Bangkok Bank has a branch here, and even the Nanyang Bank on Bonham Strand is named for the South Seas trade.

All kinds of items bought and sold

Follow Bonham Strand East along to the right. **Possession Street**, where British troops raised the Union Flag on 26th January 1841 to claim Hong Kong for Queen Victoria, leads uphill to Hollywood Road.

| Bonham Strand: busy bazaar |

| Coolies at work on the waterfront |

Claimed for Queen Victoria

Pavilions on Possession Point

Her Majesty was reasonably amused with her new possession in the Far East, but her foreign secretary, Lord Palmerston, was not: he made the famous comment that Hong Kong was "a barren island with hardly a house upon it". This had some basis in fact – at the time, the population of Hong Kong Island stood at less than 7,500 people, and a good proportion of those lived on boats in places like Aberdeen – but the founding of the colony provoked an instant influx of Chinese escaping famine, floods, typhoons and upheavals such as the Taiping Rebellion. Thousands came to make their fortune, and others came to rob them of it. By 1941, 100 years after the British stepped ashore, the colony's population had ballooned to 1.6 million.

On the right as you reach Hollywood Road, a walled garden of ponds and pavilions occupies the site of Tai Tat Tei, an open-air marketplace which served as a popular amusement ground at night. Its name was briefly revived a few years ago for the night market near the Macau ferry pier.

Hollywood Road was built by the British Army in the very earliest days of colonial administration and was named after the country estate of Hong Kong's second governor, Sir John Davis. The colony's first police station was built on the southern side of the road. It disappeared long ago but left its mark in the name of Upper Station Street.

Hollywood Road has been the first port of call for some of the best antiques to come out of China, and the street is lined on both sides by purveyors of high-quality art and curios. Or is it? You'll need to be a true connoisseur to tell the authentic originals from the well made fakes. Certainly, before the flood of Shanghainese advertising posters and Mao memorabilia washed over the street stalls of **Cat Street** just below, many relics of Qing and Ming vintage passed through the hands of Hollywood Road merchants on their way to museums and private collectors in Hong Kong and overseas. While China may now be more wary of letting its treasures leave the country, and its representatives actively try to buy them back on the international market, there doubtless remain some genuine pieces in the window displays or back rooms of shops on Hollywood Road. But for most visitors, a convincing counterfeit will do just as well.

Maoist mementoes, cultural curios

Slow-burnt incense fills the temple

Look for the ever-present tourist bus to find the incense-shrouded **Man Mo temple**. Imagine it though in early Victorian times, before the city grew up around it – surrounded by dense greenery, it would have been reached by flights of stone steps leading up from the shoreline. In those days it was also used for guild meetings and trials, and members of the temple committee gradually became recognized as unofficial representatives of the Chinese population. A plaque on the wall inside records the thanks of the Qing Emperor for donations sent from Hong Kong to help flood victims in China; evidence that Hongkongers have long been supportive of the mainland in its times of need.

Dedicated jointly to Man and Mo, the Taoist gods of literature and war, the temple's popularity extends far beyond wordsmiths and warriors. It is one of the busiest in town. Mo is better known as Kwan Yu, the red-faced god often seen in smaller shrines in restaurants. There is also an altar to Pao Kung, the god of justice brought to life in Hong Kong soap operas. Have your fortune told under the slow-burning coils of incense – the fortune-tellers speak English.

Turn right as you leave the temple. Shing Wong Street recalls the name of the city god, but any remains of a separate temple to this deity have yet to be found. However, other discoveries have recently come to light. Continue along Hollywood Road, shaded by the banyans sprouting from the fortress-like retaining wall of the disused **Police Married Quarters**. Recent excavations in the courtyard, entered from Aberdeen Street, have revealed granite foundations of what is probably the original **Queen's College**.

Then known as Central School, the college was founded in the 19th century and had a reputation as one of the best in town. One of its eminent alumni was Sun Yat-sen, revered by millions of Chinese today as father of their nation. No one was more devoted to the cause of a free and modern China than this son of Hakka peasants. By necessity he spent much of his life outside China, as an exile gathering support for revolution. His struggle against the Qing authorities was recently dramatized in the movie *Bodyguards and Assassins*.

Queen's College in its heyday...

... and a miniature of the colonnaded campus

The headmaster of Queen's College found that allowing overcrowding actually increased the school's repute: "It is an overcrowded institution which is attractive to the Chinese," he said. "If a college is half or three-quarters full, discipline suffers from the independence of parents, who think the presence of their sons a personal favour." The colonnaded school was destroyed during the Second World War and later rebuilt opposite Victoria Park in Causeway Bay, where it still stands. A detailed model of the beautiful original building has been financed by prominent businessman Stanley Ho, another successful 'old boy'.

Turbaned constables kept the peace

Central Magistracy

Hong Kong's second chief executive Donald Tsang grew up in the present-day Police Married Quarters. He comes from a police family – his brother, Tsang Yam-pui, rose to the highest rank of Commissioner. Originally marked for redevelopment, the discovery of the historic college foundations means the site will now be retained as open space – much needed in this tightly packed district.

Further along, take a look at the building at No. 60. Its upper stories are a clue as to what much of Hollywood Road must have looked like until recent decades, and its ground floor houses the beautifully old-fashioned Kung Lee tea house. You can stop and have a healthy glass of five-flower tea for $6.

Turning right here up Peel Street, a Hoklo shrine occupies half the staircase up to the Soho area of restaurants. Turn left. At the far end of Staunton Street, the grim walls of **Victoria Prison** block your way. Together with the adjoining **Central Police Station and Central Magistracy**, this collection of over twenty buildings was the nucleus of Hong Kong's law enforcement from 1841 until 2004, but now lies empty while planners consider new uses for the compound.

It was Major William Caine who instigated the building of the prison. This firebrand magistrate was so intent on upholding order in the lawless new

A walled compound of law and order

colony that he patrolled the streets himself. He set up Hong Kong's first police force, largely composed of Sikhs from Punjab, just three months after the British flag had been raised at Possession Point. These were early days in the development of policing, as London's Metropolitan Police had been formed just ten years earlier. The force quickly grew to include Europeans and Chinese. With a largely transient population, the city's crime rate was high, and no one of any wealth dared to walk the streets at night unless armed with pistols. Hong Kong remained dangerous – 384 people were convicted of highway robbery in 1866 – but thanks to the efforts of Caine and his successors, the city was a safer place by the end of the century.

Up until the handover in 1997, Victoria Prison was the oldest in use in the whole Commonwealth. It is very Victorian in character: the buildings are reminiscent of a workhouse, and the underground cells are damp, dark places. Manhole covers throughout the compound bear the stamp 'Calcutta' – relics of a time before Hong Kong industry was developed. In its final years of operation it was used mainly to house immigration offenders, serious criminals having long been shipped off to more high-security prisons elsewhere in Hong Kong.

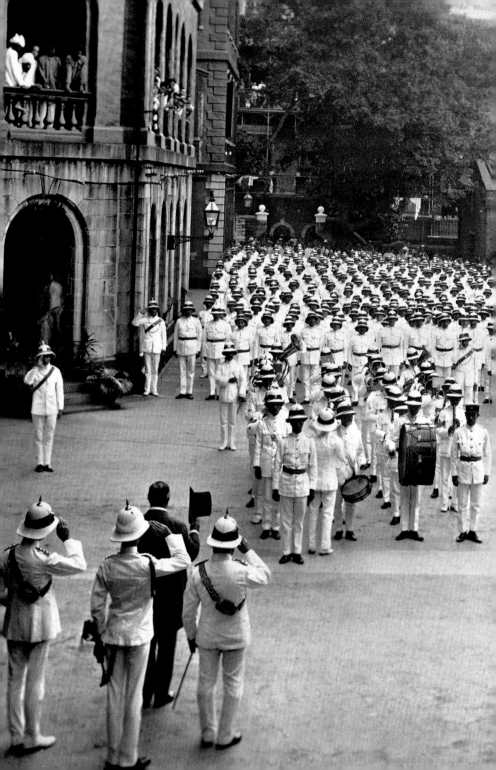

Pioneering police force: taking a salute on the parade ground

Fine frontage of the police headquarters

Old Bailey Street on its western side borrows the informal name of London's Central Criminal Court – a bailey is a fortified wall. Coming back down to Hollywood Road, you're able to admire the impressive frontage of the Central Police Station's headquarters block, built in 1919. Access to the compound is currently restricted to occasional open days, but if you're able to gain entry, you'll find that the steep access slope opens onto a parade ground surrounded by attractive buildings from various eras of Hong Kong history. The four-storey former barrack block directly opposite is the oldest, dating from 1864. The two-storey block on the right was originally the police stables.

Around the corner on Arbuthnot Road, the Central Magistracy sits atop a forbidding retaining wall which seems expressly designed to intimidate wrongdoers. Special corridors and an underground tunnel connected the magistracy to the prison, police station and exit; the passage taken by the accused after trial depended on the court's verdict.

Happier times are had at the **Fringe Club** and the Foreign Correspondents' Club, two social venues which occupy the old ice house of the Dairy Farm Company. The red-brick premises were built in the 1890s but reworked in 1913 and 1917. With its original Edwardian floor tiles in the Main Bar, the FCC is a fine example of conservation and adaptive reuse which, with any luck, will be followed by the renovators of the Police Station compound.

Opposite the FCC, at 1 Lower Albert Road, **Bishop's House** was built in 1851 to accommodate George Smith, the colony's first bishop. It may be the second oldest residence in Hong Kong after Flagstaff House. Until 1951 the building also housed St. Paul's College, but is now once again occupied by the Anglican Bishop of Hong Kong. Locally, the Anglican Church is known as Sheng Kung Hui, and runs the well regarded Diocesan Boys' and Girls' Schools. The compound contains some other attractive old buildings higher up the slope.

| Artists meet on
| Ice House Street |

| Home of Hong Kong's
| Anglican bishops |

Gaslight – a glowing reminder of the past

Follow Ice House Street downhill to the top of Duddell Street. Its stone staircase is lit at night by Hong Kong's only remaining gas lamps. In the 1840s, all European residents were required by law to hang lanterns outside their homes in an effort to light the gloomy streets and cut crime. Oil lamps were provided along the major thoroughfares, but these were seen as inadequate, and the idea of a gas company was put forward. In 1862, the Hong Kong and China Gas Company was founded as the colony's first public utility, and gas lamps illuminated the streets – making Hong Kong the first city in the East to enjoy modern street lighting.

Over the following years, all gas street lamps were phased out in favour of the electric variety, except for these four on the Duddell Street steps. This was probably because the lamp standards were custom-built for the site, and could not be converted to electricity without great expense. The gaslights thus survived to be declared monuments in 1979. Ever since then, the Hong Kong and China Gas Company – one of Hong Kong's longest established firms – has provided the fuel for them free of charge.

Bespoke lamps beautify the Duddell Street steps

As you walk by gaslight back down to Queen's Road, think perhaps of Major Caine patrolling Central with his lantern and pistol, searching the shadows for robbers to haul back to his lockup above Hollywood Road.

Around the Escalator

The steep, narrow streets above Hollywood Road bear witness to the histories of Hong Kong's Muslim and Jewish communities. Following this trail uphill will also reveal how the Qing dynasty was overthrown by Sun Yat-sen, the founder of modern China.

Start on Queen's Road Central where it meets the steps of **Pottinger Street**. It's named after **Sir Henry Pottinger**, Hong Kong's first governor, who christened the fledgling city 'Victoria'. He concluded hostilities with the Chinese and oversaw the 1842 Treaty of Nanking, which ceded Hong Kong Island to Britain, and was more prescient than most about the future of the new colony. "Within six months... it will be a vast emporium of commerce and wealth," he wrote. Pottinger became the first Hong Kong recipient of a royal honour in 1843, when he was made Knight Commander of the Bath at a ceremony in Government House.

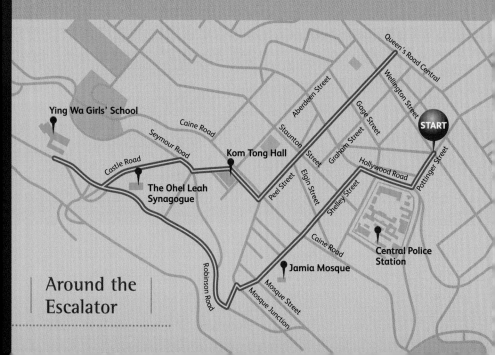

Around the Escalator

Made for sedan chairs: Pottinger Street

This 'ladder' street leads steeply uphill, and is laid with horizontal rows of roughly hewn stones for ease of ascent. Elegant women in cheongsams could switch from rickshaws at the foot of the steps to sedan chairs to be carried higher. The buildings on either side have been replaced many times, but the street is easily identifiable from old photos. It's still lined with a cornucopia of street stalls selling everything from flowers to haberdashers' supplies and fancy dress costumes. These little green sheds used to be seen all over the city but their numbers are dwindling.

As you approach the gates of Central Police Station (see page 96), turn right and join the Mid-Levels Escalator to ride up through the ever-changing restaurant scene of Soho. The next item of interest appears on your left behind a long wall.

The **Jamia Mosque** was built in 1915 by Essack Elias, originally of Bombay. Its location here made it convenient for the Muslim Indians who worked at the police station and prison on Old Bailey Street. Enter through the lovely wrought-iron gate. The mosque sits in a large, leafy compound partly occupied by ramshackle houses. The buildings opposite the mosque's entrance truly represent the old Hong Kong; more reminiscent of back-street Macau or Malacca than the modern Mid-Levels.

| Miss Hong Kong – a 1960s fashion show |

| Fancy dress stalls |

| Photo shoots on the steps |

Old-world tenements
beside the mosque

Mosque Street minaret

Wrought-iron gates

Indian influences

Hercules Robinson

Further up the escalator, turn right onto Robinson Road, named after **Sir Hercules Robinson**, governor from 1859 to 1865. **The Ohel Leah synagogue** soon appears just below street level. Built in 1902 by Jewish businessman Jacob Sassoon and named after his mother, the synagogue has an internal balcony set aside especially for women, according to orthodox tradition. The architectural style is termed Eastern Sephardic but it was designed by Leigh & Orange, a local firm which is still in business. Sir Matthew Nathan, Hong Kong's only Jewish governor, was president of the synagogue from 1904 to 1907.

By the late 1990s, Ohel Leah had been subjected to numerous inappropriate additions and alterations, and was threatened with demolition. Instead, it was renovated and returned to its original state, winning the UNESCO Asia-Pacific Heritage Award in the process. Entry is through the Jewish Community Centre next door, which also has a kosher restaurant.

Beside the glitzy entrance to 80 Robinson Road there is a small white building which attracts few glances from those passing by. It may however be the oldest building left standing in the Mid-Levels. Built in 1893, it originally housed the **London Mission**, and then from the 1930s was used as nurses' quarters by the Nethersole Hospital on the

Heritage award: Ohel Leah

slope below. Now converted into a clubhouse for the neighbouring upscale development, the elegant building is somewhat hemmed in by concrete and cement, but peek over the wall and you'll get a good view of its arched verandahs.

The Ying Wa Girls' School next door was founded by the same London Missionary Society in 1900 as a boarding school. 'Ying Wa' means 'Anglo-Chinese'. The school's uniform is a traditional blue cheongsam, and girls wearing it are an everyday sight in the area.

Coming back past the synagogue, turn left onto Castle Steps, but before you do, take a quick look at **No. 69F** on the opposite side of Robinson Road: another graceful old building which has somehow escaped redevelopment.

The London Mission

Relic of low-rise living

Cross Seymour Road and carry on down Castle Road. Here on the right stands **Kom Tong Hall**, a three-storey red-brick mansion built by **Ho Kom-tong**, the younger brother of Jardines compradore Sir Robert Ho Tung, in 1914. Ho Kom-tong needed a large home – he had 12 wives. A prominent philanthropist, he established a public dispensary further down the hill at Kau U Fong in the wake of the plague outbreak, and raised funds for the construction of the typhoon shelter at Yaumatei after the destructive typhoon of 1906. He succeeded his brother as head compradore at Jardines and eventually had more than 30 children. One of his grandsons was film star Bruce Lee, and one of his nephews is Macau tycoon Stanley Ho.

| Ho Kom-tong |

Kom Tong Hall was used by the Japanese army during World War II, and then until 2004 by the **Church of Jesus Christ of Latter-Day Saints** (the Mormons). Following an outcry which ensued when the church proposed its demolition in 2002, the property was bought by the government. It is now a museum devoted to **Sun Yat-sen**, the revered founder of republican China.

Dr Sun probably never set foot inside the building, but he and Ho Kom-tong were classmates at Queen's College in the 1880s, and when Dr Sun began his efforts to overthrow China's corrupt Qing dynasty, Robert Ho Tung was one of the Hong Kong people who provided support. Dr Sun and his comrades in the revolutionary 'Revive China Society' met and conspired in places on Hollywood Road, Gough Street and Staunton Street, and a Sun Yat-sen Trail links some of these locations to the museum.

Sun's statue outside his museum

Large family residence: Kom Tong Hall

Father of the nation, Sun Yat-sen

Presidential quill and seal

Dr Sun's calligraphy brushes

"The question I am often asked is where did I get my revolutionary and modern ideas," Dr Sun told students at the University of Hong Kong many years later. "The answer is that I got my ideas in this very place... I saw the outside world and began to wonder how it was that foreigners, that Englishmen could do such things as they had done, for example, with the barren rock of Hong Kong, within 70 or 80 years, while China in four thousand years had no place like Hong Kong... I saw that it was necessary to give up my profession of healing men and take up my part to cure my country."

Sun travelled widely – as far afield as Japan, Singapore, London and Hawaii – to gain support for his anti-imperial campaigns. The museum displays some interesting and touching letters written by him during the revolutionary period, and explains the eventual founding of the Republic of China through photographs, papers and other artifacts.

"It will be your pleasure to hear from me that I have assumed the Presidency of the Provisional Republican Government in China," he wrote to his friend James Cantlie in January 1912, "which I accepted with disinterested fervour in order to render myself an instrumentality to rescue China with its four hundred million population from environment of impending perils and dishonour." Still, although the Manchu emperor was forced to abdicate, fighting with regional warlords went on well into the 1920s.

A statue of Sun stands outside the museum. Uniquely among 20th-century political leaders, his memory is revered by the governments of both China and Taiwan; the official calendar in Taiwan takes 1912 as its starting point, and Zhongshan Roads in most Chinese cities are named after Sun's birthplace in the Pearl River Delta.

To finish, carry on across Caine Road, turn right and make a left turn under the bridge. Here you may meet the umbrella repairman, a character who has become a minor local celebrity in recent years. Peel Street takes you steeply back downhill to Central.

The umbrella man of Peel Street

Around Victoria Barracks

The continued existence of the Prince of Wales Building (now known as the People's Liberation Army Hong Kong Building) in Central is a reminder that the military have always maintained a presence in the centre of town. The Royal Navy's dockyard long occupied everything north of Queensway, giving Admiralty its name, and the British Army kept barracks on extensive lands to the south of the road. Follow this route to discover colonial buildings, air raid tunnels and other fascinating remnants of local history.

The Hong Kong Government had a longstanding complaint that the city's growth was constricted by the twin army and navy bases. Queensway and Kennedy Road were bottlenecks as the only links between Central and Wan Chai. Naval land was thus surrendered in 1959 for the construction of a new road to link the two districts. This was fittingly named after a naval figure: Sir Cecil Harcourt, the admiral of the British fleet which liberated Hong Kong in 1945. Victoria Barracks, the separate army fiefdom, was handed over to the government in its entirety in 1979 and its site is now occupied by Pacific Place and Hong Kong Park.

HMS Chatham oversaw the British withdrawal in June 1997

St. John's Building, above the lower Peak Tram terminus

Queen's Road Central

Harcourt Road

Lower Albert Road

Upper Albert Road

Garden Road

Cotton Tree Drive

Flagstaff House Museum of Tea Ware

High Court

Queensway

Government House

START

Lower Terminus Peak Tram

Pacific Place

Helena May

World Wildlife Fund Headquarters

Visual Arts Centre

Hong Kong Park

Supreme Court Road

St.Joseph's College

Zetland Hall

Edward Youde Aviary

Justice D

Kennedy Road Station

Union Church

Kennedy Road

British Consulate

St. Paul's College

Office of the Former Chief Executives of the HKSAR

Explosives Magazine

Macdonnell Rd.

Borrett Rd.

Kennedy Road

Bowen Road

Hong Kong Electric Cen

| Around Victoria Barracks |

Barrack blocks: when all of Admiralty was military

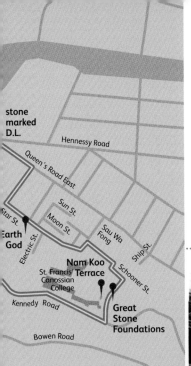

This walk starts at the lower terminus of the **Peak Tram**. Even without a ticket you can step inside and see some of the original steam-driven machinery. The first winding engine which pulled the carriages uphill may have been built by one of the local shipbuilding firms, but the iron wheels and gears for the later electric system were sourced from the Metropolitan-Vickers company of Manchester.

| *Ascent to the Peak in 1934* |

Behind and to the left of the terminus, the **World Wildlife Fund** has its local headquarters in a tiny building beside the tram line. Over the tracks you can see the rear of the **Helena May**, the entrance to which is on Garden Road. It's an imposing Edwardian building which was opened in 1916 as a residence and club for single expat women, and it has retained that general purpose to the present day. It was named after the wife of the then-governor, Sir Henry May, who had been Chief of Police before rising to the highest office. In 1912, when the couple returned to Hong Kong after a posting in Fiji, Helena

The grand old lady of Garden Road

dodged a bullet meant for her husband. An aggrieved man whose father had been imprisoned by May attempted to assassinate the new governor near the old GPO on Pedder Street, but the bullet lodged in Helena's sedan chair and no one was harmed. Like Chris Patten, Henry May brought a coterie of daughters to Government House.

The Helena May lost its extensive library during the war – much of which had been censored by Lady Clementi, the prudish wife of another governor, who rejected all books which hinted at any hanky-panky – but the collection has been rebuilt.

Gunman apprehended

Family May...

... and Family Patten

On your left, the blue-and-white school with twin bell towers is the **Catholic St. Joseph's College**. This 1920s-era building was originally the premises of the Club Germania, but the German property was confiscated by the government after the First World War and passed to the La Salle Brothers, who still run the school.

Take the footpath uphill and then turn through the striped archway to reach the **Kennedy Road station** of the tramway. Not many people use the intermediate stops these days. You can tell whether the tram is coming, and from which direction, by watching the movement of the steel cable. With the variations in Hong Kong's climate, the cable expands and contracts, varying the stopping position of the carriage at each station by up to a metre.

Saved by the bell: St. Joseph's College

The tram crosses a quiet Kennedy Road in the 1940s

Today's leafy route is little changed

雍 仁 會 館
ZETLAND HALL
No.1 KENNEDY ROAD
HONG KONG

THIS STONE WAS LAID BY
RIGHT WORSHIPFUL BROTHER CHARLES BERNARD BROWN
DISTRICT GRAND MASTER - ENGLISH CONSTITUTION
AND
RIGHT WORSHIPFUL BROTHER ARTHUR ANDERSON DAND
ON J.G.W. DISTRICT GRAND MASTER - SCOTTISH CONSTITUTIO

IN THE PRESENCE OF MANY BRETHREN
ON THE SECOND DAY OF APRIL A.D.1949 A.L.5949.

Zetland Hall, home of the lodge

Masonic foundation stone

Beside it at 1 Kennedy Road stands
Zetland Hall, the discreet location
of Hong Kong's Masonic Centre.
The Freemasons have met here
since 1950, after their earlier lodge
on Zetland Street was destroyed in
an American bombing raid in 1944.
The fraternity has been present locally
since the earliest days of British settlement:
the Royal Sussex Lodge was established here in

Emblems of office: pocket watches and a collar jewel

1844, followed by Zetland Lodge in 1846. Chinese members were admitted
from the 1890s onwards, after the Qing authorities relaxed their restrictions,
and Freemasonry spread across the region. One of the first Chinese Masons in
Hong Kong was Sir Kai Ho Kai, the businessman who reclaimed the land that
became Kai Tak.

All lodges in China were closed down after 1949, but many relocated to Hong
Kong, and there are currently 29 local groups which meet under the auspices
of the Grand Lodges of England, Ireland and Scotland. Some retain the names
of their original treaty port home towns, such as Amoy, Foochow and Swatow.
Membership is drawn from the realms of business, law, government and
particularly the police force. A universal condition of joining is the belief in a
supreme being, but the nature of this being is left open to interpretation, and
the order states that Freemasonry is not a religion, nor a substitute for one.

Opposite, the interdenominational **Union Church** was founded in 1890, according to its foundation stone, but the current buildings date from 1954. To its left, the buildings of St. Paul's College stretch uphill to Macdonnell Road. The institution was founded in 1915, and was the first co-educational school in Hong Kong, introducing the revolutionary idea of educating boys and girls together. These buildings date from 1927.

Harbour view:
Union Church
in 1890

St. Paul's College,
co-educational pioneer

28 Kennedy Road

The handsome mansion at 28 Kennedy Road, somewhat hidden by a large tree, dates from the early 20th century and has been a bank, a school and a residents' club. In the 1990s it served as offices for the Joint Liaison Group, the intergovernmental body tasked with finalizing arrangements for Hong Kong's handover of power. The house performed a function of unique historical significance, providing an accessible location for the lengthy, complex discussions.

On the 29th of May 1997, after 15 years of intense work, all members of the British JLG were asked to assemble beneath the Royal Arms in the ballroom at **Government House** for the last governor, Chris Patten, to join them in a commemorative photograph. The coat of arms, of a design dating back to the Norman conquest, was dismounted and immediately after the handover installed in the newly-opened British Consulate-General a short distance away. There it remains today, complemented in its new location by artist Ju-ming's wooden sculpture *Tai Chi*. The Kennedy Road mansion now has a new purpose as the **Office of the Former Chief Executives of the HKSAR.**

Chris Patten shares a joke with the Joint Liaison Group

The Royal Coat of Arms today – in the British Consulate

Arched verandahs of Cassels Block

Kennedy Road is bordered for much of its length by the green domain of **Hong Kong Park**, formerly Victoria Barracks. The colonnaded Cassels Block, which was built in the early 1900s as army married quarters, extends down the hillside. Its conversion into the **Visual Arts Centre** was inaugurated in 1992 by Ronald Leung Ding-bong, the then-chairman of the Urban Council, who was affectionately known as Dr. Toilet for his promotion of clean public conveniences. The Urban Council, an elected public body with full autonomy from the government – and an annual budget larger than that of many Chinese provinces – was abolished in 1999 by Tung Chee-hwa, and its many municipal and cultural functions divided among government departments; a reversal of grass-roots democracy which went unnoticed by many. Its once-ubiquitous pink bauhinia emblem is now a rare sight.

Sir Edward Youde

Keeping to the higher footpath through the park brings you to the **Edward Youde Aviary**, named after Hong Kong's only Welsh governor, who died in office in 1986 while negotiating the terms of the future handover. He was a popular figure in Hong Kong and thousands of people turned out for his funeral parade from Government House to St. John's Cathedral. His hearse was an army jeep. The walk-through aviary recreates a rainforest, with tall canopy trees and 600 exotic birds.

The governor's cortège arrives at St. John's

Down the hill, Rawlinson House is another military building which has been converted for other uses – in this case, a marriage registry which processes new couples at great speed. On the other side of the ornamental lake, a bronze statue of a soldier is identified as John Robert Osborn of the Winnipeg Grenadiers. In fact the statue was originally cast by the Eu family to represent a First World War soldier, and was placed in the gardens of their house Eucliffe at Repulse Bay. When the house was demolished, the statue was donated by the family to the British Army and stood for some time in Osborn Barracks in Kowloon Tong before being moved to Hong Kong Park.

Unknown soldier?

John Osborn is worthy of remembrance though and it's fitting that a statue even erroneously attached to his memory should stand in these former military grounds. Osborn was born to a gypsy family in Norfolk but emigrated to Canada in 1920. He fought near Wong Nai Chung Gap in 1941 (see page 216), finally flinging himself upon a grenade to save the lives of his comrades, and was awarded the Victoria Cross for his heroic self-sacrifice. This remains the only VC awarded in Hong Kong.

Flagstaff House is one of the oldest Western buildings remaining in the territory. Known as Headquarters House until 1932, it was built in Greek Revival Style in 1846 by the Royal Engineers as the residence of Major-General George D'Aguilar, the Officer Commanding Her Britannic Majesty's Land Forces in China. Its deep verandahs are well suited to the local climate, and the building was the venue for regimental cocktail parties

attended by officers and wives in dress uniform and formal attire. It remained the residence of the Commander of British Forces until 1978, when it was handed over to the government along with the rest of Victoria Barracks.

Today it is the **Flagstaff House Museum of Tea Ware,** and displays the extensive collection of Dr. K.S. Lo. Some items date back as far as the Western Zhou dynasty (1045–771 BC). Tea has a special place in Chinese culture – consider the traditional wedding ritual of serving tea to parents – and a cup of tea unites the British and Chinese as few other things can. The museum holds tea appreciation classes every week.

Tea connoisseur: Dr. K.S. Lo

Flagstaff House, the Major-General's residence

Venerable banyan preserved at great expense

Hong Kong Park exits onto the High Court and Pacific Place. Just past the Island Shangri-La Hotel, there's a large **banyan tree** which may be 140 years old. When Swire Properties purchased the former military land to build Pacific Place in the 1980s, the government stipulated that this tree should be preserved. While the steep hillside was excavated for the construction of the five-level shopping arcade and underground car park, the tree was supported in a giant concrete plant pot 18 metres wide. This cost HK$23 million, and is thought to be the world's most expensively preserved tree.

The excavations also uncovered hidden underground bunkers, the most important of which was the Combined Services Operating Headquarters, better known in wartime as the 'Battle Box'. This subterranean complex of war rooms, similar in concept to Winston Churchill's command centre under London, was reached by a long flight of steps from the barracks. It was from here that General Maltby directed the defence of Hong Kong in 1941. The rooms were last used during the street riots of 1967. To allay fears of disturbed souls from the war years, Taoist monks were brought in to perform exorcism ceremonies.

Opposite the **British Consulate**, officially opened by Princess Anne amid lion dances in January 1997, a thickly forested stream valley contains another collection of old military buildings long deserted by their original owners.

Princess Anne officiates at the opening of the Consulate

THESE BUILDINGS
WERE OFFICIALLY
OPENED BY
HER ROYAL HIGHNESS
THE PRINCESS ROYAL
ON 30TH JANUARY
1997

荷蒙
安妮公主殿下親臨

為此數幢大樓主持啟用禮

爰綴數言以垂永紀

一九九七年一月三十日

Military relics hidden in the greenery

GG Block was once the home of the British Army's Special Investigation Branch. Now it has been renovated to serve as the entrance to the US-based Asia Society's Hong Kong centre, which spans the valley and opened in 2012. Further up, the compound encircled by a wall was the **Explosives Magazine**. The three low buildings are separated by mounds of earth to limit the effects of any explosions, and tram tracks for moving materials around the site still exist. There's an Admiralty anchor symbol on the gatepost with the date 1910, but the buildings inside probably date from 1843 to 1874. The area from here down to Queensway used to be known as Queen's Lines.

The underpass leading to the Hong Kong Electric Centre is a very good example of very bad design. Not only is it totally out of keeping with the green surroundings and the old walls of the explosives depot, but it is paved with such slippery materials that permanent signs are required to warn you not to fall over. So mind your footing as you ascend to Kennedy Road and turn left.

After passing **St. Francis' Canossian College**, with its wall mural of angels, take a flight of stairs down into an old and largely forgotten part of town. Great stone foundations with balustrades are all that remains of the once-grand **Tung Chi College**.

Foundations of a
good education:
Tung Chi College

Comfort house:
Nam Koo Terrace

The graceful red-brick mansion known as **Nam Koo Terrace** has fared slightly better. It was built between 1915 and 1921 in Colonial Eclectic style for a Shanghainese merchant family. Despite its European influences, which include arched windows and an attractive colonnaded porch, the placement of its entrance gate and a Chinese pavilion on the roof suggest it was laid out in accordance with *feng shui* principles. During the Japanese occupation it was used as a 'comfort house', or brothel, for soldiers, and it has a reputation for being haunted. It is many years since the house has been lived in, so its generally good condition is a testament to its standards of construction. Notably, no alterations appear to have been made over the years, so Nam Koo Terrace is a prime candidate for preservation.

Take the first left onto Schooner Street – like Ship Street, a reminder of the days when this old neighbourhood was nearer the waterfront. Stairs lead up to **St. Luke's College**, another building abandoned since the 1980s, although this one is a little more puzzling since it is modern.

Sau Wa Fong leads onto Star Street, which passes the short stub of Electric Street – site of Hong Kong's first power station, the light from which possibly inspired the local street names of Sun, Star and Moon – before you find a tiny **earth god shrine** in an alley to your left. This has been here for a century or more, but the red pennant hanging above

The earth god of Star Street

it is more recent. Look behind the shrine and you'll see a door leading into the hillside. This connects to a system of air-raid shelters built into the hills behind Wan Chai prior to the Second World War. The original portal to this tunnel was further forward, but the Star Crest development excavated part of the hillside, potentially rousing the spirits of people who are said to have been executed in the tunnels; hence the red banner as a measure to soothe their souls.

Where Queen's Road East meets Queensway, three more tunnel entrances front onto the street. Originally built as air-raid shelters, they were used until recently to store low-level radioactive waste from hospitals. The two tower blocks on the hill above them, Dragon House and Paget House, are still army barracks so it's unlikely the tunnels will be opened up for public use. There is another major network of wartime tunnels and portals at the other end of Queen's Road East, beneath Wah Yan College.

Defence Lot: boundary of the old barracks

Take a look at the post with a **stone marked D.L.** (Defence Lot) and the iron railings which stretch on for a short distance. Rather bizarrely, this is all that's left of the once-extensive Queensway frontage of Victoria Barracks, and it's hard to see why it alone survived. The squat 1970s building behind the railings used to be the guardroom to the east gate of the barracks.

At the main entrance to Pacific Place, under the pedestrian walkway, you can still see where the road and tram line used to make a sharp right-angled turn. Here, in the 1970s, the Immigration Department occupied one of the old army buildings, and each morning the pavement was crowded with hundreds of new immigrants who had crossed the border from China and wished to declare their arrival. Until 1980, the 'touch base' policy meant that any illegal immigrant who successfully reached the urban area was allowed to stay in Hong Kong; but if they were caught in the New Territories, they were sent back to China. Today, some of the busy commuters waiting in line at the bus stops may well be reenacting the queues made by their parents a generation ago.

New Hongkongers line up at Queensway to register their arrival

Government Hill

The major religious and governmental institutions of colonial times took root on the foothills above Queen's Road, and the area once known as Government Hill is still peacefully green and leafy. Follow this route to visit graceful buildings and gardens from an earlier age.

Start beside the Fringe Club at the top of Ice House Street. Narrow Glenealy leads uphill into the Mid-Levels; follow it through an underpass beside heavy retaining walls to discover a hidden Roman Catholic enclave. Up on the right, behind the Caritas buildings, stands Hong Kong's Cathedral of the Immaculate Conception. Built in 1888 after occupying earlier premises on Wellington Street, it is completely surrounded by high-rise buildings and most people pass by unaware of its existence.

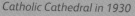
Catholic Cathedral in 1930

Government Hill: a green precinct beside the business district

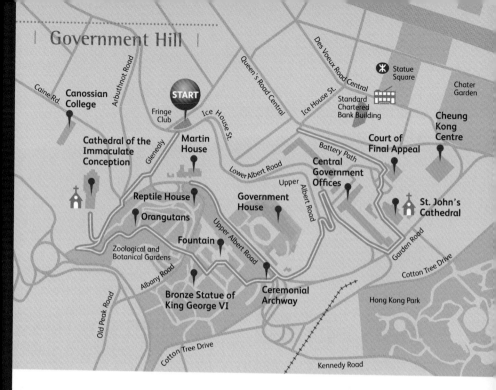

The Gothic-style cathedral owes its founding to one Theodore Joset, a Swiss priest stationed in Macau in the late 1830s. Catholic soldiers in Hong Kong – probably Irishmen – had appealed for a priest to minister to their fever-stricken fellows. Joset was faced with a dilemma: the request had to be met, but he was in Macau as a guest of the Portuguese establishment, which was protective of its control of religious affairs on the China coast. His plea for a spare priest was rejected, and so he appealed directly to the Vatican, which granted his request with a decree removing Hong Kong from Macau's jurisdiction. Communications in those days were slow and Joset was able to keep this under his hat for the best part of a year, but when the news finally broke, there was uproar and he was ordered to leave the Portuguese colony within 24 hours. He sailed over to Hong Kong and held services in a mat-shed church before work on a permanent building was started in 1842.

Because of the direct link to Rome, Italian missionary societies have played a key role in the local Catholic community. The Canossian College further along Caine Road was originally known as the Italian Convent.

The cathedral's altar of **St. Joseph** was a gift from King Victor Emmanuel II of Italy, and bears the royal arms of the House of Savoy. The building's Italian connections helped it avoid much of the looting suffered by other churches during the Second World War, since Japan was not at war with Italy.

The botanical gardens in 1925

Glenealy itself was once known as Elliot Valley, after Charles Elliot, the Chief Superintendent of British trade in China who orchestrated the seizure of Hong Kong but found himself dismissed for procuring such a useless island. Unlike most subsequent leaders (Chris Patten a notable exception), he is commemorated by no local place names.

Go back down the drive to enter the gate of the **Zoological and Botanical Gardens**, which were initiated by **Sir John Bowring** (1854-1859) and opened to the public in the 1860s. The location is still a cool, shady oasis of exotic trees and flowers. The primary aim of the gardens was to increase knowledge of indigenous plants and thereby speed the work of afforesting Hong Kong Island, for in those days, people scoured the hillsides for firewood and grass and the 'barren rock' did indeed appear quite bare. Bowring, the fiery fourth governor, was a polyglot who was popular with the locals for his unusual ability

Sir John Bowring

to speak Chinese, as well as for his actions to build schools and appoint Chinese members to the Legislative Council; but his reputation was marred somewhat by his eager involvement in the Arrow War against China, which ended with Kowloon and Stonecutters Island being added to the young colony.

He and Lady Bowring both suffered from the ingenious terrorist act perpetrated by the **E Sing Bakery** of Wan Chai: arsenic was added to all the

Veteran resident

bread baked on the morning of January 14th, 1857, in an attempt to murder the city's entire European population at breakfast. It might have succeeded were the dose not so high, but the excess amount of arsenic caused vomiting rather than death, and the plot was foiled. There was no evidence to convict the owner of the bakery, but he was deported anyway. A kindred spirit lives on today in the form of the Mid-Levels dog poisoner, who has yet to be caught despite leaving portions of poison-laced chicken along Bowen Road for the past 20 years.

Poison plot: the Wanchai Bakery

At the **Reptile House**, there's a huge Burmese python – a snake which is native to Hong Kong. A flight of steps leads up to the mammal enclosures. The stars of the show here are the ring-tailed lemurs and a pair of orangutans. Siu Fa, the jaguar which lived in the gardens for two decades, died in 2008. A subway takes you under Albany Road to the older half of the park, which houses tropical birds and a greenhouse.

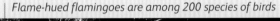

Flame-hued flamingoes are among 200 species of birds

Anton Chekhov, the Russian dramatist, visited Hong Kong in 1890 and was rather impressed with it: "It has a glorious bay, the movement of ships on the ocean is beyond anything I have seen in pictures, excellent roads, trolleys, a railway to the mountains, museums, botanical gardens."

The unassuming pavilion is the oldest structure in the gardens; it was donated by the Parsee community and was used as a bandstand for Sunday concerts. At the top of a flight of steps, a bronze statue of **King George VI** – the father of the current Queen Elizabeth – marks the 100th anniversary of Hong Kong's founding. The lower section of the gardens is centred around a **fountain**, a popular leisure spot with tree-fringed views of the familiar tall buildings of Central. Bear right at the fountain to leave the gardens through a **ceremonial archway** dedicated to all the Chinese who fought in the world wars.

Memorial archway

1950s vista of Government House and the harbour

Botanic bronze: King George VI

Government House: home to 25 British governors, two Japanese lieutenant-generals and one chief executive

High society gathered at garden parties on the lawns

The Japanese-styled tower of **Government House**, residence of Hong Kong's governors and now of its chief executive, stands out across the road, preceded by flower beds. The main building dates from 1855, and Bowring was the first to move in. Prior to this, governors had to live in rented premises, unlike the army chief and the taipans of the trading hongs who had palatial mansions built for themselves. Even the humble colonial chaplain had his own house. When it was completed, Government House boasted a 60-foot ballroom and a staff of blue-gowned servants to match, and the cream of high society would come to hobnob at frequent parties. New-fangled electric fans were introduced in 1908. It overlooks the business heart of Hong Kong, although its original harbour views are now blocked by acres of reclamation. Today, the building and grounds are opened to the public on several days per year. At other times, you can get a glimpse inside if you pass on the top deck of a bus.

Last waltz: the final year of British rule

Historic events have taken place at Government House. The Japanese surrender was received within its walls in September 1945. At the height of the Cultural Revolution, crowds of leftists waving little red books chanted slogans at its gates. And of course, on a rainy day in 1997, Hong Kong's final governor and his family departed the building for the last time before attending the handover ceremonies.

1945: the Japanese surrender documents are signed at Government House

1997: well-wishers gather at the gates for a farewell glimpse of the Pattens

INSTRUMENT OF SURRENDER.

We, Major General Umekichi Okada and Vice Admiral Ruitaro Fujita, in virtue of the unconditional surrender to the Allied Powers of all Japanese Armed Forces and all forces under Japanese control wherever situated, as proclaimed in Article Two of the Instrument of Surrender signed in Tokio Bay on 2nd September, 1945, on behalf of the Emperor of Japan and the Japanese Imperial Headquarters, do hereby unconditionally surrender ourselves and all forces under our control to Rear Admiral Cecil Halliday Jepson Harcourt, C.B., C.B.E., and undertake to carry out all such instructions as may be given by him or under his authority, and to issue all necessary orders for the purpose of giving effect to all his instructions.

Given under our hands this 16th day of September, 1945, at Government House, Hong Kong.

In the presence of

On behalf of the Government
of the United Kingdom.

On behalf of the Commander-in-Chief,
China Theatre.

海軍中將

藤田類太郎

陸軍少將

岡田梅吉

Instrument of
surrender

The original appearance of Government House

The Oriental revisions to the building's architecture – including the balconied tower – date from the Second World War, when the occupying lieutenant-generals lived there; but the internal Japanese features were removed at the end of the war. Government House has been used to accommodate state visitors, such as Lady Thatcher, Queen Margrethe of Denmark, and Diana, Princess of Wales. Since 1997, the 19th-century royal coat of arms, which originated in the British legation in Peking and then graced the Government House ballroom for many years, has been relocated to the British consulate in Admiralty.

Autographed portraits of state visitors

To the left of Government House, **Martin House** is home to the deans of St. John's Cathedral. Han Suyin, the Eurasian author of *A Many-Splendoured Thing*, once lived there. Only half of the building remains: the western part was severely damaged in a typhoon in the 1950s and replaced with a utilitarian block of apartments.

Martin House in its entirety

The remaining east wing

The first Colonial Secretariat, popular with termites

Its colonnaded replacement lasted only 30 years

The present-day offices, graced by the same rosewood tree

Cross the street to follow Upper Albert Road around the back of Government House, for better views of its tower and gardens. Black-and-white bollards mark a short cut down to Lower Albert Road – both named for Queen Victoria's beloved prince consort. You emerge right in front of the simple yet elegant **Central Government Offices**.

The civil administration of Hong Kong has been headquartered here since 1848. The first tropical-style two-storey building was completed in the early 1850s, but it coped poorly with the local humidity and white ants, and was demolished in the 1920s in favour of a colonnaded building with enclosed upper floor offices. This was in turn replaced in 1953 by the present eight-storey **Government Secretariat**. A large Burmese rosewood tree has stood in the central courtyard for many years, its branches shading generations of protesters – at least until the time of the handover, when a high steel fence was thrown around the entire compound. These buildings were vacated in 2011 when the shiny new government headquarters at Tamar were opened, and this leafy, low-rise space – a great asset in this crowded district – is now subject to a tussle between citizens' groups, who want to keep it, and the government, which wants to redevelop half of it.

St John's Cathedral:
an oasis of calm

Turn right and follow the pavement to enter the compound of **St. John's Cathedral**. This strangely peaceful pocket of land in the middle of Central is the only freehold in the entire SAR; all else is leased.

The first stone of the Anglican Cathedral was laid in 1847, and the building has barely changed since the chancel was extended in 1873, but much of its visible history has a distinctly wartime flavour. The interior took a lot of flak during the years of occupation – all the stained glass windows were lost when a shell hit them in their place of storage – so all are post-war. The window depicting a merchant seaman and local fisherwoman was inaugurated in 1959 to remember all those who lost their lives at sea during times of conflict. The current bells in the tower were presented by the Hongkong Bank on the occasion of Queen Elizabeth's coronation in 1953, and a native white-bellied eagle is represented in part of the floor mosaic.

Stained-glass fisherwoman

St. John's seen from
Garden Road in 1947

St. John's has had close links with the various military units which have defended Hong Kong. The now-tattered colours of the Royal Air Force, the Hong Kong Auxiliary Air Force, the Hong Kong Naval Reserve and the **Hong Kong Volunteer Defence Corps** (otherwise known as the Royal Hong Kong Regiment) are laid up in St. Michael's Chapel on the south side. The Regiment's colours were hidden during the occupation. Marked with the battle honour 'Hong Kong', they were laid up here in 1971 and will, by tradition, remain among other regimental memorabilia until they disintegrate.

Memorial tablets to the Middlesex Regiment, and a record of tablets which did not survive the war, are found on the wall. A simple **brass crucifix** on a wooden board was originally mounted in the chapel of the Sham Shui Po prisoner-of-war camp (see page 348). It has become a tradition to place flowers before it in nothing fancier than a jam jar, as was done in the camp.

On the central aisle of the Cathedral, the first pew facing the **lectern** bears a royal crest; before the handover, this row was reserved for the Governor or any visiting royal. Until the 1920s, the effects of the tropical climate were tempered by sets of swaying punkahs fixed to the rafters – an Indian

The Queen's colours of the Royal Hong Kong Regiment

Carved relic of wartime worship

invention imported from the Raj to help air circulation. The Anglican diocese of Victoria (as it then was) originally encompassed most of the Far East, including all of China, Korea and Japan, but as new bishoprics were established the diocese shrank to just Hong Kong and Macau. Today, the Cathedral looks after three 'daughter' churches at Pokfulam, Discovery Bay and Stanley (St. Stephen's).

Outside the church, a single soldier is buried close to where he fell in December 1941. Private Maxwell was in fact a Catholic, but access to the cemeteries must have been difficult in the heat of war, and so he was buried in the nearest suitable place. Every year a Michaelmas Fair is held in the grounds, with proceeds going to welfare schemes around Hong Kong.

The front pew, reserved for the sovereign

St. John's overlooked the military parade ground

The French Mission, now the Court of Final Appeal

Eroded emblem

Crest of the Missions Etrangères

24 . MARS . 1917.

Li Ka-shing's Cheung Kong Centre is built on the site of the old Hilton Hotel, which brought the sixties swinging into Hong Kong when it opened in 1963. Although the basement bar had to shorten its name to 'The Den' – because the government of the day wouldn't allow the word 'opium' to be used – it still featured waitresses squeezed into provocative mini-cheongsams. And during

Sir Robert Brooke, Air Chief Marshal, inspects Gurkha troops in 1941

that long summer of streetside queues for water, the hotel scored brownie points by keeping its swimming pool dry. Despite its popularity, the Hilton lasted barely 30 years before being replaced by the current office tower. *Cheung Kong* is Cantonese for 'Long River', i.e. the Yangtze.

Before the Hilton, the site was for many years a military parade ground. Perched above it on Battery Path, and outliving most of its neighbours, the attractive red-brick building is currently Hong Kong's **Court of Final Appeal**. It previously housed the French Mission; a crest on the south wall marked **M. E.** *(for Missions Etrangères)* is dated 1917, but the building had many owners and uses before then. Sir Henry Pottinger, Hong Kong's first governor, may have lived there in 1843; it was owned by Emmanuel Belilios, the chairman of the Hongkong & Shanghai Bank, in the 1870s; it later served as the Russian consulate; it was pressed into service as the seat of the provisional Hong Kong Government in 1945; and was later used as the home of the Education Department, Victoria District Court and the Government Information Services. It remains to be seen whether buildings like the Cheung Kong Centre will last as long.

You can walk down Battery Path and take a bridge across Queen's Road into the Standard Chartered Bank Building. Statue Square, with its tram stops and MTR entrances, is on the building's far side.

Central

Almost all of the people involved in Hong Kong's early days as a British settlement are remembered in the street names of Central, then and now the city's commercial and administrative hub. A walk through the district tells the story of the city's evolution from colonial backwater to major trading port.

This walk starts at Exit D1 of Central MTR station. As you step onto Pedder Street, you'll find the Pedder Building on your right, a rare survivor from the 1920s. The building is well maintained, though the stone gargoyles above its ground-floor arches fell off in the 1990s. Sedan chairs once waited where taxis now line up across the road. The locally founded Shanghai Tang department store, which made its name by reviving the styles of pre-war Shanghai, occupied the lower two floors for many years until it was recently ejected by the landlord – one more homegrown icon which has had to give way to demand for yet more imported luxury brand names. The long-established China Tee Club was also given its marching orders.

| *Shanghai chic: the classic cuts are back* |

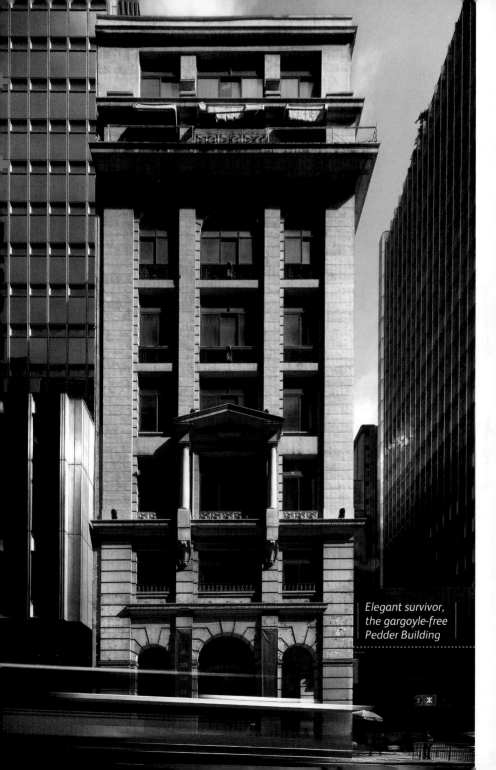

*Elegant survivor,
the gargoyle-free
Pedder Building*

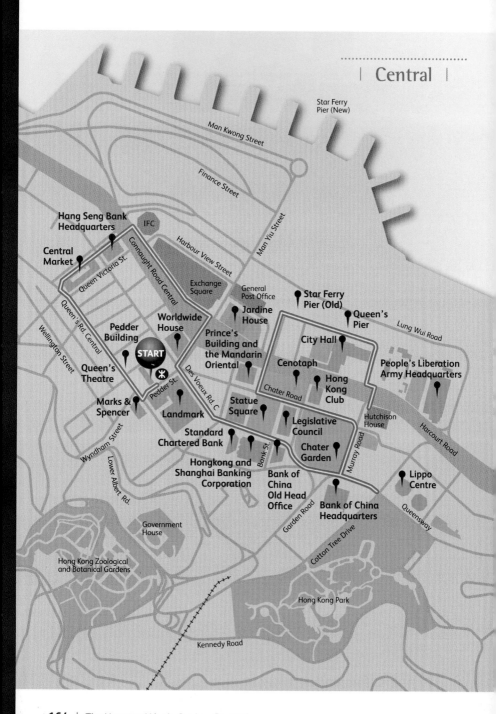

Star Ferry Pier (New)

Man Kwong Street

Finance Street

Man Yiu Street

Hang Seng Bank Headquarters

IFC

Central Market

Connaught Road Central

Queen Victoria St.

Harbour View Street

Exchange Square

General Post Office

Star Ferry Pier (Old)

Queen's Pier

Lung Wui Road

Queen's Rd. Central

Wellington Street

Worldwide House

Pedder Building

Jardine House

Prince's Building and the Mandarin Oriental

City Hall

Cenotaph

People's Liberation Army Headquarters

START

Queen's Theatre

Pedder St.

Des Voeux Rd. C

Hong Kong Club

Statue Square

Chater Road

Marks & Spencer

Landmark

Legislative Council

Hutchison House

Harcourt Road

Wyndham Street

Standard Chartered Bank

Bank St.

Chater Garden

Murray Road

Lower Albert Rd.

Hongkong and Shanghai Banking Corporation

Bank of China Old Head Office

Lippo Centre

Government House

Bank of China Headquarters

Queensway

Garden Road

Hong Kong Zoological and Botanical Gardens

Cotton Tree Drive

Hong Kong Park

Kennedy Road

Hong Kong Park

Lapraik's clock tower on Pedder Street

At the top of Pedder Street, where Marks & Spencer's mannequins look out from their shop windows, stood an **ornamental clock tower** which chimed its first hour on New Year's Eve 1862. It was a gift to the young city from one of its most successful taipans, Douglas Lapraik, builder of Douglas Castle in Pokfulam. Perhaps the gesture was a nod to his start in life as a watchmaker. The clock had a reputation as perhaps not the best judge of time, but its illuminated dial was a useful night-light to guide boats to the wharf at the foot of the street. Pedder Street was named after William Pedder, the first Harbour Master. Like Temple Bar on the Strand in London, the clock tower was eventually condemned as a traffic hazard and it was demolished in 1913.

Turn right at the **zebra crossing** – a fearsome mass of interweaving businesspeople during office hours – to proceed down Queen's Road Central. Originally a muddy track running along the waterfront, and later called Main Street, it was renamed in honour of Queen Victoria in 1842.

It has long been the main commercial artery of Hong Kong. Pictures from the 1860s show graceful colonnaded buildings such as the King's Theatre and **Queen's Theatre** on either side of a **tree-lined** avenue, although it changed in alignment and appearance as it entered Sheung Wan – here it became more Chinese in character, snaking between open-fronted shops, balconied tenements and busy street markets.

The road has never declined in commercial importance, and today it is lined by banks, hotels, department stores, grade-A office towers and high-end shops of all kinds. On your right, "the Lanes", parallel alleyways full of narrow-fronted

King's and Queen's – long-lived theatres

shops and street stalls, provide a more down-to-earth shopping experience than the international **brand-name stores** on the main road.

Queen Victoria Street – yet another namesake of the long-lived monarch in this parcel of land sandwiched between Victoria Peak and Victoria Harbour – borders the Central Market. This Bauhaus-style structure, built in 1939 and vacated by the meat and vegetable traders in 2003, was much admired for its streamlined design which makes the most of natural light and ventilation. It has recently been saved from the wrecking ball and will be converted into a 'green oasis' for the area's office workers.

Billboards and businesspeople

Take the stairs up to the first floor and walk through the market's arcade. This was created in the early 1990s to link up with the Mid-Levels Escalator, and will probably be removed to restore the original atrium of the market. The walkway leads you across Des Voeux Road Central – named after **Sir George Des Voeux**, Governor from 1887-1891, and mispronounced by everyone – and through the first floor of the **Hang Seng Bank** headquarters. Hang Seng got into financial trouble in the mid-1960s and was rescued by HSBC, who still run it today. The bank has given its name to Hong Kong's stock market index.

George William Des Voeux

| *Hang Seng HQ* | | *Portholes in reflection* |

Noble House: Jardines set new heights for Central's 1970s skyline

Turn right before the entrance to IFC to carry on along the elevated walkway. This section is packed with foreign domestic helpers on Sundays, some of whom arrive early in the morning to stake out their patch. Passing Exchange Square and turning right onto the bridge over Connaught Road, you have a view of Jardine House and its distinctive portholes. Known as the Connaught Centre when it was opened in 1973, it was then the tallest building in town, dwarfing everything else and dragging Hong Kong into the age of skyscrapers. Its round windows were inspired by the traditional moon gates of Chinese gardens.

The swashbuckling history of Jardine, Matheson & Co. – which originally involved the trading of opium, among many other commodities – was dramatized by James Clavell in a series of novels. A hammy 1980s television adaptation of *Noble House* is great fun to watch. Jardines is the only surviving firm that was doing business in the area before Hong Kong was founded in 1841. It was once said that colonial Hong Kong was ruled by Jardines, the Jockey Club and the Governor, in that order. Times have changed, but the 'princely hong' is still run by Scots, and it is still Hong Kong's largest employer after the government.

Mail was delivered by boat to the GPO

Worldwide House over the road, now a warren of remittance centres and Southeast Asian food shops, is built on the site of the old **General Post Office**. This striped red-brick curiosity was built in 1911 – using plans which were intended for the GPO in Nairobi but sent to Hong Kong by mistake, according to rumour – and was demolished in 1976 for the construction of the MTR.

Descend to ground level and follow the zebra crossings over to the Landmark. **The Hong Kong Hotel**, the colony's first luxury lodging house, was built upon this waterfront site in 1892. It had all the mod cons, including "hydraulic ascending rooms of the latest and most approved types which convey passengers and luggage from the entrance hall to each of the five floors above." Monthly room rates started at HK$45.

Most of Central's core commercial area is built on reclamation – hence the straight roads, flat land and large plot sizes when compared to more inland neighbourhoods. Much of the early reclamation was initiated by **Sir Catchick Paul Chater**, the Calcutta-born Armenian tycoon who founded the Hong Kong Land company in 1889. His large-scale Praya Reclamation Scheme commenced two years earlier, pushing the city's waterfront 75 yards further out into the harbour and adding 65 acres of valuable land to the district.

Sir Catchick Paul Chater

The old praya, or promenade, became Des Voeux Road, and the new praya was named Connaught Road after Queen Victoria's second son, the Duke of Connaught, who visited Hong Kong in 1890. The new harbourfront lots were quickly occupied by colonnaded office buildings, godowns and private jetties, and the city took on the elegant appearance of Shanghai's Bund.

The Hong Kong Hotel beside Pedder's Wharf

Further down Des Voeux Road you'll find the headquarters of **Standard Chartered Bank**. This British institution, which still does most of its business in Asia, was founded by James Wilson, a Scottish Member of Parliament who also established the *Economist* newspaper. Wilson was a great proponent of global free trade. In 1853 he was granted a Royal Charter and established the Chartered Bank of India, Australia and China to develop trade with the East. This business mushroomed with the opening of the Suez Canal in 1869 and the extension of the telegraph lines to China in 1871.

Thanks to its charter, the bank was allowed to issue its own banknotes, something it still does today. In 1969, as the winds of independence were blowing through the colonies of Asia and Africa, it merged with the Standard Bank of British South Africa to become Standard Chartered.

The bank's second building in Hong Kong, a fine example of Colonial Italianate, was built on the nearby corner of Duddell Street and Queen's Road in 1871. George Duddell – an opium farmer and land auctioneer who became rich by the simple method of selling lots to himself at bargain prices – was the previous owner of the site, and had apparently secured the property and three adjoining lots for the paltry sum of one pound and ten pence. Standard Chartered has occupied its current address since 1933.

Royal charter: former head office of the Chartered Bank

Next door, the headquarters of the **Hongkong and Shanghai Banking Corporation** have stood on the same prestigious site – 1 Queen's Road Central – since it was founded in 1865. No other bank has been so closely connected to the fortunes of Hong Kong as the locally based HSBC. In a city which hosts hundreds of financial institutions, many of which have branches on every main street and in every shopping mall, everyone knows which one you're referring to when you say 'the bank'.

In its earliest days, Hong Kong had no currency of its own, and merchants used Chinese silver bullion and Mexican dollars for trading. **The Hong Kong dollar** was introduced only in 1864. British banks with operations in India and Malaya opened branches in Hong Kong, but the business community wanted a bank with local headquarters. A consortium of European merchants therefore founded the Hongkong and Shanghai Bank – 'a bank in China more or less founded on Scottish principles'. This locally based institution was better able to serve the particular needs of the China Coast trade, and it was an immediate success: within 18 months it had opened branches in Bombay, Yokohama, London and San Francisco. The bank began to issue banknotes straight away.

Hong Kong dollars through the years

Sir Vandeleur Grayburn, the Hongkong Bank's chief manager, decided in the 1930s that it was time to replace the 1886 building which was beginning to show its age. A contract to design the third head office on this site was thus awarded to the local architects Palmer & Turner – with the instructions to build 'the best bank in the world'. To ensure an uninterrupted supply of materials, as the building made use of large quantities of stone and marble, the bank purchased an entire quarry and invested in a brickworks. The new

The new headquarters stood head and shoulders above the business district

headquarters towered above the city and attracted world attention upon its opening in 1934. Standing 220 feet high, it was the tallest building in Asia, and its monolithic granite façade was the height of art deco design. Its Queen's Road entrance was topped by a portcullis and guarded by great bronze doors. The curved mosaic ceiling of the banking hall, impressive in height and detail, portrayed merchants and workers of all races engrossed in symbolic labour. Its interior walls and columns were finished in green, cream and black marble and the building was fully air conditioned – a rarity at the time. Guarded by a pair of bronze lions, the effect was one of great authority and financial strength.

The Bank: symbol of stability

Until the 1930s Hong Kong was still a low-rise city, where most buildings rose no higher than four floors, and were colonnaded with wide verandahs, high ceilings and overhead fans. The bank's new headquarters set the tone for the modern age and quickly became recognized as a symbol of Hong Kong's wealth and stability.

The following decades saw great expansion as the bank bought other operations such as the Mercantile Bank and the British Bank of the Middle East, becoming in the process one of the world's largest financial groups. By the 1970s the famous head office could cope no longer. The decision was made to replace it with something entirely different.

Stephen and Stitt on the move

Sir Edward Youde and Michael Sandberg inaugurate the new building

Architect Sir Norman Foster proposed a radical departure from the stern, imposing style of previous buildings. Instead of looking like a fortress, the **new headquarters** should show a transparently open, public face, and inspire affection rather than awe. Built at a cost of over HK$5 billion – the most expensive building project in the world at the time – the high-tech marvel features steel masts supporting a series of diagonal trusses, each two storeys deep, with suspended floors whose unobstructed interiors are drenched in natural light reflected from an external mirror. Escalators angled to conform to geomantic precepts carry customers up into a vast atrium. When it was unveiled in November 1985, just one year after the signing of the Sino-British Agreement on Hong Kong's future, the new building was seen as a reassuring statement of the venerable bank's faith in its home city.

Now several reclamations back from the harbour, it nevertheless retains its view out to sea. The site holds spiritual significance in the *feng shui* atlas of Hong Kong: the mountain dragon's *chi* flows from the Peak, down through Government House to the sea, via 1 Queen's Road Central.

Stephen and Stitt, the **bronze lions**, are named after two managers of the bank. They received shrapnel damage, still clearly visible, during World War II. They have only been moved twice: once to Japan during the occupation, where they luckily avoided being melted down for armaments; and then over the road to Statue Square while the new headquarters was being built.

Hallowed ground: angled escalators follow feng shui principles

Like Jardines, both banks have Scots origins

Across Bank Street, the old head office of the Bank of China completes the trio of banks which issue Hong Kong dollar banknotes. Completed in 1950, shortly after the Communist Party came to power on the mainland, it was created by the same architects who had designed the neighbouring Hongkong Bank building of 1934. Palmer & Turner were commissioned to ensure that the Bank of China exceeded its local rival in height, while emulating its granite-faced dependability. A heavy vault door, ordered from the United States, was never delivered because of the introduction of a United Nations embargo on trade with China following its entry into the Korean War in 1950. Legend has it that the door still gathers dust in some North American warehouse.

The old Bank of China

In 1967, when Hong Kong was subjected to a brief overspill of rioting from the Cultural Revolution, the Bank of China bristled with loudspeakers inciting revolution against the colonial authorities. Cricketers played on regardless as propaganda boomed across the cricket ground opposite. The bank was a Maoist citadel in the heart of capitalist Central. At one stage – perhaps to guard against the possibility of raid by helicopter – the bank's roof was covered with metal structures and barbed wire.

The chaos of the Cultural Revolution came to an end in 1976 with the deaths of Chairman Mao and the more moderate premier Zhou Enlai. Queues of people quietly waiting to pay their respects wound through several blocks of Central.

Pre-war glamour: the China Club

Today, the old Bank of China preserves the art deco style redolent of Hong Kong's past. Its heritage role is further enhanced by the evocative old-world charm of the **China Club** which occupies its upper floors. The club's library and dining rooms hark back to the golden age of 1930s Shanghai.

Exiled guardians

The bank's front doors are guarded by two stylized lions of the kind which are often seen outside Chinese temples – but walk around to the building's eastern side to see a more unusual pair. These **art deco lions** were designed by Palmer & Turner, but were rejected by the bank managers of the day as 'too reactionary'. They were subsequently banished to the University of Hong Kong campus for several years.

Returning to HSBC's bronze lions, cross the tram lines to enter **Statue Square**. This open area, originally known as Royal Square, was part of Chater's 1890 reclamation and has been a focal point of the city ever since. When it was first laid out, statues of Prince Albert, Queen Victoria and Edward VII all stood in the square. Perhaps appropriately, in this city which values commerce above all else, the only one remaining in place is an effigy of Sir Thomas Jackson, the chief manager of the Hongkong and Shanghai Bank from 1870 to 1902.

On the left-hand side, **Prince's Building** and the **Mandarin Oriental** were originally Prince's Building and Queen's Building: a matching pair of grand, four-storey piles with arched verandahs, porticoes and corner turrets. On its completion in 1899 on the then waterfront, Queen's Building was the city's most desirable address. In the 1960s, in response to demand for modern office space and for hotel rooms to meet the new boom in worldwide holiday travel, both buildings were redeveloped into their current form. They were linked by what was to become the first of many pedestrian bridges between buildings in Central. At the same time, the government beautified the square with sculptures, paper-bark trees and fountains, creating the peaceful open space it is today – a good place to take a break from office work or from a day of sightseeing.

Prince's and Queen's Buildings looked onto Royal Square

On the opposite side of the square, the neo-classical granite building originally built for the Supreme Court housed the **Legislative Council** from 1985 to 2011. Look up and you will see a figure of **blindfolded Justice** above the royal crest on its pediment. Chinese influences include a double layer of roof tiles. The architects, Webb & Bell, were also responsible for London's Victoria and Albert Museum and the frontage of Buckingham Palace. At the court's opening in January 1912, the Chief Justice rather presciently declared: "When Victoria has ceased to be a city, when the harbour has silted up, when even the Hong Kong Club has crumbled away, this building will remain like a pyramid to commemorate the genius of the Far East." Less than a century later, his predictions have more or less come to pass.

In the run-up to World War II, Hong Kong's shorelines were protected by barbed wire, mines and gun emplacements, but only a few important buildings were sandbagged. The Supreme Court was one of them. Nevertheless the building's columns sustained some damage during the street fighting in 1941, and this can still be seen.

Sword and scales – rule of law

Sandbags surround the Court

Statue Square: Queen Victoria and the Supreme Court

Harcourt assembles a post-war judiciary

In October 1945, upon the reoccupation of Hong Kong, Rear Admiral **Sir Cecil Harcourt** reconvened the Judiciary in the Supreme Court building. A military administration ran Hong Kong until the Governor, Sir Mark Young, returned in May 1946 and civil government was resumed.

Chater Garden and the Legislative Council today

The local legislature moved into the building in 1985, and the square has since been the site of many political protests. Pro-democratic lawmakers led a chant for democracy from its balcony on the evening of June 30th 1997, hours before the midnight handover – the next day, a provisional legislature was put in place with fewer elected members. In early 2010, ministers and pro-government legislators were trapped inside the building by an angry crowd of young protesters during a controversial vote on the massively expensive Express Rail Link to Guangzhou. The legislature moved to the new Tamar government headquarters in 2011; one wonders whether a purpose-built escape tunnel for unpopular politicians has been included in the plans.

Behind the building, Chater Garden was laid out in 1978 on the former grounds of the Hong Kong Cricket Club. It's a pleasant garden of fountains and flame trees. Cricket was played here for 124 years before the authorities decided this prime plot could be put to better use. From here you have a good view of the current Bank of China headquarters, successor to the 1950 head office. The innovative structure was designed by architect I. M. Pei. For him, the job held great emotional significance as his father had been the bank's first Hong Kong manager of the Nationalist era. The only recognizably Chinese aspect in his striking design is a two-ton granite base reminiscent of Beijing's ancient city gates, but the tall, slender building took a bamboo sapling – revered by Chinese as a symbol of strength and endurance – as its inspiration. The topping-out ceremony took place on the auspicious date of 8th August 1988.

I.M. Pei

Bamboo inspiration – the Bank of China

Twin towers: Lippo Centre

The Hong Kong Club

Further towards Admiralty, the equally distinctive **Lippo Centre** was opened in the same year by later-disgraced Australian financier Alan Bond. The design is supposed to emulate koalas climbing a eucalyptus tree.

The **foundation stone** of Chater's 1890 reclamation is now located in Chater Garden. To the north, the premises of the Hong Kong Club overlook the Cenotaph. In the days of empire, colonial clubs were the hubs of social life – but only for the right sort of people. Founded in 1846 and modelled on similar establishments in Madras and Calcutta, the **Hong Kong Club** was initially located on Queen's Road, where the Entertainment Building now stands. Monthly subscription fees were $4.

Chater's reclamation: grand buildings and monuments graced the waterfront

In 1897, club members moved to a magnificent new building on reclaimed land nearer the waterfront. The imposing four-storey building was in the Italian Renaissance style, with a grand teak staircase. "The new Club stands in a commanding situation on the praya with an unobstructed view of the harbour to the north side and of the Peak on the south, so that it is in an excellently fine position to catch the summer breeze," said the *China Overland Report*.

An extraordinary general meeting in 1980 saw the membership divided on the question of whether to preserve or demolish the Victorian clubhouse. Despite a petition to Queen Elizabeth, the venerable building was torn down. Its replacement, opened in 1985, preserves an aura of genteel refuge from the demands of one of the world's busiest cities. But change still comes slowly to the Hong Kong Club: it only opened its doors to women in 1996.

Walking back to **Statue Square**, you pass the **Cenotaph**, a memorial unveiled in 1923 to honour all those who died during the Great War and later reinscribed to add those who defended Hong Kong during World War II. It is

Black Watch at the Cenotaph

based on an identical monument in London designed by Sir Edwin Lutyens. In the final years of British rule, the flags of Hong Kong, the Army, Navy and Air Force were raised and lowered at the Cenotaph by kilted Scottish troops of the Black Watch.

Out of respect for the fallen, the lawn around the Cenotaph is out of bounds except during remembrance services – but this rule was spontaneously broken during June 1989, when the monument became a gathering point for thousands of people expressing their grief for those killed on Tiananmen Square.

Follow the underpass from Statue Square towards the waterfront. Until 2006, this ended at the concourse of the **Star Ferry pier** – but the much-loved landmark was demolished, to widespread anger and dismay, in favour of a six-lane harbourfront highway.

The government was perhaps taken unawares by the depth of public feeling for the pier and its immediate environs. Until the first cross-harbour tunnel was opened in 1973, generations of Hong Kong people used the Star Ferry daily on their way to and from work. Everyone had memories of Edinburgh Place, the plaza adjoining the pier. Besides commuters, it was used by tourists, anglers, pleasure boaters, dating couples and wedding photographers. It was a true public space, a rare asset in a crowded city of narrow streets, and an accessible piece of the waterfront.

During November 2006, tens of thousands of people streamed to the Star Ferry pier to cover it with their own photos, sketches and essays of what it meant to them. A new phrase – 'collective memory' – was on everyone's lips.

Pier pressure: police remove determined protesters

Around 150,000 people visited on the last day of its operation. Protesters began a month-long sit-in. It was a strange reprise of the Star Ferry protests of 1966, when a fare rise triggered a five-day riot. It was also a sign of the changing times: that event had been anti-colonial in nature, while the new protest was aimed at preserving what remained of the past. So Sau-chung, the hunger striker who spurred that protest 40 years earlier, stopped by to lend his support to the demonstrators.

On December 12th, after demolition workers broke through the crowd to enter the site, some protesters – including radical legislator Leung Kwok-hung, or "Long Hair" – occupied the pier to stop its destruction. A struggle between the police and the demonstrators ensued before the government was able to demolish the clock tower and the rest of the building three days later.

Combined with a growing perception that the government favours the interests of big business over the general public, and colludes to hand common areas over to private developers who already control too much wealth, the event critically damaged the credibility of the Hong Kong government.

Sticking to its guns, for it had already awarded contracts to construction companies, the government went ahead with the demolition of the neighbouring **Queen's Pier** in 2007. Again, crowds turned out to defend the historic structure.

Queen's Pier, where new governors and visiting dignitaries traditionally first set foot on Hong Kong soil, had been conceived as a cohesive part of Edinburgh Place. Ron Phillips, the man who had designed its third incarnation in the 1950s, added his voice to calls for its preservation. "This building and the surrounding areas were to be for everyone," he said. "Any loss of such an amenity will be a disaster."

"Like many people in Hong Kong, we would be sad to see this familiar landmark go," added the British consulate. But such words fell on deaf ears. In the face of even greater opposition than with the Star Ferry demolition – radicalized activists established themselves in tents on the roof of the pier, and were removed only with great difficulty by some 300 police officers – the government went ahead and demolished the structure.

One good thing came out of the debacle: the idea that Hong Kong people didn't care for their heritage was shattered. Henceforth, every proposal to demolish historic buildings has been met with vociferous opposition, primarily from young people.

Queen's Pier: Elizabeth II steps ashore in 1986

Set back from the former location of Queen's Pier, **City Hall** was built in 1960 in the same uncluttered style as the Central Government Offices on Lower Albert Road. Between the two blocks, a remembrance garden has bronze gates dedicated to the Hong Kong Volunteer Defence Corps. With concert halls, exhibition galleries and libraries, City Hall greatly invigorated the cultural life of the city when it opened. Its harbour-view dim sum restaurant is a popular place to *yum cha*, or 'drink tea'.

Beyond City Hall, the local garrison of the People's Liberation Army is headquartered in a walled compound formerly known as **HMS Tamar**. This is the remaining portion of the Naval Dockyard, which once occupied a much larger area – its basin was reclaimed in the 1990s to form the land for the new government offices. The base was a thorny issue in the handover

The Naval Dockyard occupied a vast area east of Central

Prince of Wales Building: the PLA's base in Hong Kong

negotiations: the British were keen to relocate all military units away from the city, but the PLA insisted on staying put. Now cut off from the harbour, naval vessels are located instead at a purpose-built base on Stonecutters Island.

The narrow-waisted headquarters building was opened by the Prince of Wales, and named after him, in 1979. A pedestrian bridge over Connaught Road gives you a better view into the military compound, although it seems to be occupied by only a skeleton staff. The bridge leads into Hutchison House, and from here you can connect to the Central-Admiralty walkway system.

So Kon Po and Causeway Bay

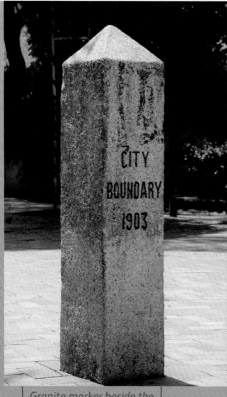

Granite marker beside the racecourse

Most people visit the So Kon Po neighbourhood behind Causeway Bay only when the annual Rugby Sevens are in progress. At other times, it's a quiet and somewhat old-fashioned area pleasant for walking, and you can follow an easy route through Tai Hang and Victoria Park.

Take any tram or bus bound for Happy Valley and alight on the long straight stretch of Wong Nai Chung Road before you reach the stone ramparts of St. Paul's School. One of the **old city boundary stones** – dated 1903 – stands on the pavement outside the racetrack, and Broadwood Road leads quickly uphill to **St. Margaret's Church**.

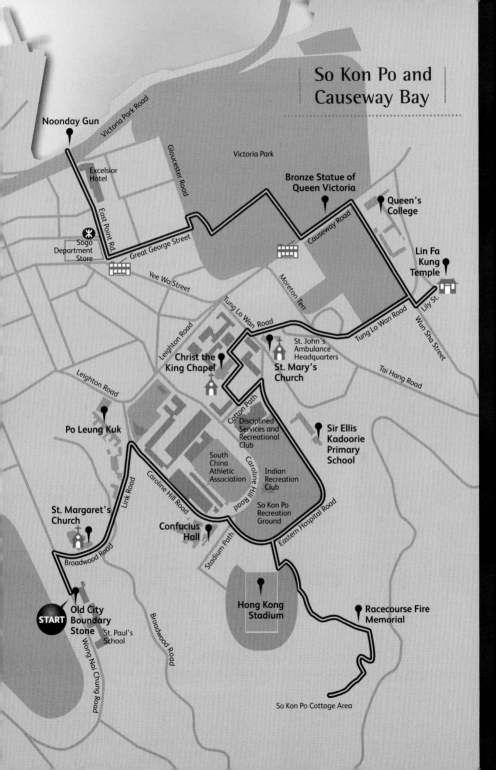

So Kon Po and Causeway Bay

Noonday Gun

Victoria Park Road

Victoria Park

Gloucester Road

Excelsior Hotel

East Point Rd.

Bronze Statue of Queen Victoria

Queen's College

Causeway Road

Sogo Department Store

Great George Street

Lin Fa Kung Temple

Yee Wo Street

Moreton Terr.

Tung Lo Wan Road

Wun Sha Street

Lily St.

Leighton Road

Christ the King Chapel

St. John's Ambulance Headquarters

St. Mary's Church

Tung Lo Wan Road

Tai Hang Road

Leighton Road

Cotton Path

Disciplined Services and Recreational Club

Po Leung Kuk

Caroline Hill Road

South China Athletic Association

Caroline Hill Road

Indian Recreation Club

Sir Ellis Kadoorie Primary School

Link Road

So Kon Po Recreation Ground

Eastern Hospital Road

St. Margaret's Church

Confucius Hall

Stadium Path

Broadwood Road

Hong Kong Stadium

Racecourse Fire Memorial

START Old City Boundary Stone

St. Paul's School

Wong Nai Chung Road

Broadwood Road

So Kon Po Cottage Area

*Graceful columns
announce
St. Margaret's*

天主教堂

ST. MARGARET'S CHURCH
聖瑪加利大堂
地址: 2A BROADWOOD ROAD

The church was built in 1923 to serve the Roman Catholic community of the Happy Valley area, and its Greek-style frontage has been a local landmark ever since. It has a handsome bell tower at the back, and a grotto hidden beside it. Follow the road over the hump and down the other side of the hill. The compound of the **Po Leung Kuk** occupies all the land on your left.

This charitable group was originally founded in 1878 to stop the trade in *mui tsai*, or servant girls. 'Po Leung' means 'protect the innocent'. At the time, the abduction of young girls for indentured servitude in wealthy households was commonplace. The custom only died out completely in the early 1970s.

The Kuk has since widened its remit to take care of children's education and social services for the elderly, and a post on its committee is considered evidence of high social standing. One of the halls on the site is named after Kwan Tai, the Chinese historical figure known for his sense of righteousness. The main art-deco building of the Po Leung Kuk dates from 1932.

| Po Leung Kuk archway |

| Hall of Confucian learning |

Double back to follow Caroline Hill Road southwards. Like Morrison Hill Road, the name recalls a former hill which has long since been flattened for development. Opposite the premises of the South China Athletic Association, which has its own popular football team, the **Confucius Hall school** is built in traditional Chinese style.

Past this, you arrive at the **Hong Kong Stadium**, home of the Rugby Sevens and other major sporting events.

There has been a sports stadium here since the 1950s. In those days, it was called the Government Stadium and, despite having no roof, was the venue for all the city's most important football matches. It was redeveloped into its current form in 1994 with the intention of hosting concerts as well as sporting events, but noise complaints from nearby residents put a stop to that.

The wooded hillsides around it were covered with squatter villages built by new migrants from China. These were only cleared in 2001, and you can still follow paths uphill on either side of the stadium to explore their remaining terraces and foundations. Besides rubble and staircases to nowhere, you can find hundreds of old brown San Miguel bottles from the days when the beer was brewed locally. Were the squatters big drinkers? Possibly, but the sturdy bottles were also used to reinforce the cement walls and floors of their makeshift homes – truly, the beer that built Hong Kong.

Capacity crowd at the city's main stadium

Spot the local: expats out in force for the rugby

To the left of the stadium, clearly signposted, a considerable flight of steps leads up through the fenced-off remains of old villages to an unexpected sight: the imposing **Racecourse Fire Memorial**, built in 1922 to commemorate the people who died in the February 1918 fire at the Happy Valley racecourse.

This event was one of Hong Kong's worst disasters. "The races afforded great pleasure – the Chinese are as much excited as the English and bet with much ardour," reported the *Illustrated London News*. Accordingly, a large crowd had gathered for Derby Day. But a cooked food stall sparked flames which quickly consumed the tinder-dry matshed stand erected for the spectators, and in little more than 20 minutes, over 600 people trapped in the collapsed structure were dead.

Surrounded by bamboo forest and built of granite slabs, and including pagodas, pavilions, arches and balustrades, the memorial is a pleasing spot.

Garden of remembrance in bamboo forest

Being slightly overgrown only adds to its charm. The hillside on which it stands is still called Coffee Gardens on some maps, after a 19th-century plantation which briefly existed here.

Back downhill, carry on past the grounds of the Indian Recreation Club, passing several long-established schools. **Sir Ellis Kadoorie Primary School** was originally known as the Ellis Kadoorie School for Indians. It was the first school in Hong Kong where Indian languages were used in teaching, although many of the pupils were Eurasians and local Chinese. At one time, due to overflowing demand, the school was run in morning and evening shifts.

The Kadoories were Baghdadi Jews who came to Hong Kong in the 1880s from Bombay. They quickly succeeded in business, and the family still owns a clutch of local concerns including the Peninsula Hotel, the Peak Tram and China Light & Power.

| Tranquil memorial |

IN MEMORY
OF THOSE WHO
PERISHED IN THE
RACE COURSE
FIRE ON
FEBRUARY 26TH
1918

本
山
后
止

Derby disaster: matsheds ablaze at Happy Valley

Hidden heritage: Christ the King Chapel

Sisters of the French Convent

Passing on your left the spacious, well-manicured playing fields of the Disciplined Services and Recreational Club, turn left onto Cotton Path, once the site of a cotton mill. Here behind a high wall, in the grounds of St. Paul's Convent, stands **Christ the King Chapel** – one of Hong Kong's most imposing but least known historical buildings. You're free to walk in. Built in 1928, the large domed church is supported by columns of impressive size.

Like St. Margaret's in Happy Valley, it's a Catholic church. The order of nuns which run it, the **Sisters of St. Paul de Chartres**, came to Hong Kong from France in 1848. One of

Orphans left in the nuns' care

their first acts was to establish an orphanage to care for children abandoned because they were girls, because they were sick or because their parents were too poor to keep them. Word soon spread, and abandoned infants started appearing on the convent's doorstep instead of being left on the streets.

Today, there is no more need for the orphanage, but the order still operates a prestigious girls' school and hospital on the premises, both referred to locally as 'French', and the sisters in their black-and-white habits still run the show. Prominent alumni of St. Paul's Convent School include Christine Loh and Dame Lydia Dunn, who have occupied posts in Hong Kong's Legislative and Executive Councils.

Western religion, Eastern style

You can exit through the hospital onto Tung Lo Wan Road. 'Tung Lo Wan' or 'Copper Gong Bay' is the Chinese name for Causeway Bay. On your right, **St. Mary's Church** is built in a perhaps-overdone Chinese style – probably to reassure prospective converts who might have thought, on the evidence of other church buildings, that Christianity was too Western. It dates from the 1930s, as does the St. John's Ambulance Headquarters just further on. This charitable organization has been operating in Hong Kong since 1884.

Carry on past the bus station to Wun Sha Street and make a left turn down Lily Street, which ends at the attractive **Lin Fa Kung temple**. Unlike most other Chinese temples, which are of a standard design, this one is unique, being octagonal in shape. It is dedicated to Kwun Yam, or Guanyin, the Buddhist Goddess of Mercy. This popular deity originated in India as Avalokitesvara,

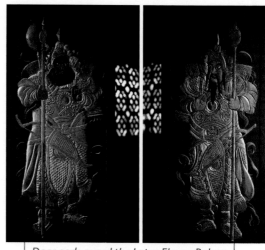
Door gods guard the Lotus Flower Palace

Unique design: Lin Fa Kung

a male god, but somehow became seen as female after crossing the Himalayas. 'Lin Fa Kung' means 'Lotus Flower Palace', and the temple holds dozens of lotus flower lamps.

Backtrack down Lily Street to the old neighbourhood of Tai Hang Village. These streets play host to the annual Fire Dragon Dance, a well attended event which is held around the time of the Mid-Autumn Festival. The three-day event commemorates a 19th-century outbreak of plague which was eradicated after a goddess appeared to the Hakka villagers and instructed them to perform the dance. In thanks, or perhaps in the practical view that prevention is better than cure, it has been performed annually ever since. The snaking dragon, held aloft by up to 50 people at a time, dances to the beat of drums and carries thousands of sticks of smouldering incense. Giant joss sticks are carried alongside to add to the billowing smoke. The effect on a hot, steamy evening is oppressive but primal in its intensity. It's well worth a visit.

The name 'Tai Hang' refers to a watercourse which used to empty into the sea near here. Return to Tung Lo Wan Road to follow a channelled remnant of the stream through the grounds of Queen's College. This path takes you to Causeway Road, which once formed the waterfront.

Qing-attired students of Queen's College

Queen's College dates from the earliest days of colonial Hong Kong, but its fine 19th-century building was destroyed during the Second World War. It has stood on the current site since 1950. Sir Alexander Grantham, Governor of the day, laid the **foundation stone**. The open playing fields have been used by the school since 1897.

The foundation of a good education

The college was the first Anglo-Chinese Secondary School in Hong Kong – designed to draw the best from Western-style education and Chinese culture. Its stated mission has not changed since it was founded in 1862: 'to spread brilliant boys all over China and to strengthen the country's youth'. Girls were admitted for a brief time, but today it has reverted to being a school for boys only. The foundations of the college's original Central premises were recently uncovered on Hollywood Road (see page 95).

Cross the road to enter Victoria Park, laid out in the 1950s on land newly reclaimed from the typhoon shelter. Its centrepiece is a seated **bronze statue of Queen Victoria** herself. This was originally located on Statue Square in Central, where it was erected for her Diamond Jubilee of 1897. This marked an unprecedented 60 years on the throne – a time in which she oversaw a vast expansion of the British Empire. A jubilee procession in London included troops from every British colony, together with soldiers sent by Indian princes; Victoria was also the Empress of India. The Victoria Cross, or VC, was introduced in 1856 by Queen Victoria to reward acts of valour, and it remains to this day the highest British and Commonwealth award for bravery.

During the Second World War, all public statues were shipped to Japan to be melted down for the war effort. However, upon the war's end, Victoria's statue was found mostly unharmed in a Japanese scrapyard and was returned to Hong Kong. It was restored and placed in its new location in 1952. The statue was splashed with red paint in 1996

Statue Square: original location

Victoria's Park

*Crimson queen:
definitely not amused*

by disaffected artist Pun Sing-lui, who then proceeded to cover himself with paint as well; the stunt earned him a month in jail.

As Hong Kong's largest open space, Victoria Park hosts the annual Lunar New Year Fair, a crowded event at which people buy flowers and other items for the coming new year. Midnight is the busiest time. Since 1990, the park has also been the venue for the annual candlelight commemoration of the Tiananmen Square massacre – or 'incident' in more diplomatic terms. Whatever the label, Hong Kong remains the only place in China, Macau included, where the events of June 1989 can be publicly remembered.

On Sundays, Victoria Park is frequented by thousands of foreign domestic helpers, primarily from Indonesia – their counterparts from the Philippines prefer to gather in Central. Leave the park by its western exit to join Great George Street. This leads to a junction with Yee Wo Street, where the Sogo Department Store overlooks what may be Hong Kong's busiest pedestrian crossing. Trams nudge their way through a sea of teenage trendsetters, or fashion victims, depending on your age and point of view.

East Point Road leads off north from here. It's hard to imagine the past in such a frenetic setting, but this area once housed the godowns and stables of Jardine Matheson & Co., Hong Kong's 'princely hong'. In fact, this seafront lot was the very first site sold at the colony's very first land auction in 1841. A mansion for the taipan – known as Number One House – was built on a rise overlooking East Point, and was surrounded by trees and manicured gardens.

All this has disappeared, except for the grand **stone archway to the Jardine stables** – this was taken apart many years ago and reassembled at the Beas River Country Club near Fanling in the New Territories. Yee Wo Street, however, preserves the hong's Chinese name.

Garden gateway: Causeway Bay in quieter days

The gate now graces the Beas River Country Club

From the underground car park of the Excelsior Hotel – which stands on the site of Lot No. 1, and is still owned by Jardines – a tunnel leads beneath Gloucester Road to the harbourfront site of the **Noonday Gun**. This three-pound Hotchkiss cannon is fired daily at noon, and also – to the tinkle of champagne glasses – at midnight at the New Year. Jardines have been firing it every day for a century and a half, but so much mythology has developed around it, it's hard to tell why.

Some say the company was commanded to fire the gun every day by the Royal Navy as punishment for having greeted an arriving taipan

| *Noel Coward fires off the noonday gun* |

with a cannon salute. The reality may be that the Royal Navy had fired a noonday gun every day from early in Hong Kong's history, to assist ships in the harbour with their timekeeping. In 1870 the service was discontinued as part of a cost-cutting exercise, and Jardines may have decided to reinstate it as a public service. Today, the firing of the noonday gun has long been superfluous to the shipping trade, but it's become a ritual daily event that even Noel Coward commented upon in *Mad Dogs and Englishmen*: "In far Hong Kong, they strike a gong, and fire off a noonday gun".

From here it's a brief walk back to the MTR, or tram line, at Yee Wo Street.

| Jardines staff do the honours daily |

Wong Nai Chung Gap

The pass, or gap, between Happy Valley and Repulse Bay is used daily by thousands of commuters and tourists. But Wong Nai Chung Gap also played an important role during the Second World War: as a meeting of five roads at the midpoint of Hong Kong Island, it was a crucial position to hold, and it saw some of the fiercest close-quarters fighting of the Battle of Hong Kong. This short walk – which has recently been signposted with the help of the Canadian Consulate – takes you back to those desperate days.

War sites are marked by the Canadian government

Untested Canadian troops on training exercises in Hong Kong

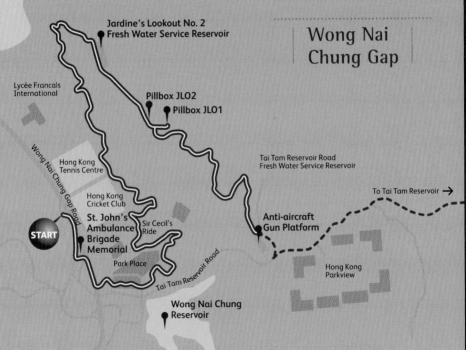

Jardine's Lookout No. 2
Fresh Water Service Reservoir

Wong Nai Chung Gap

Lycée Francals International

Pillbox JLO2
Pillbox JLO1

Wong Nai Chung Gap Road

Hong Kong Tennis Centre

Tai Tam Reservoir Road
Fresh Water Service Reservoir

To Tai Tam Reservoir →

Hong Kong Cricket Club

St. John's
Ambulance
Brigade
Memorial

Sir Cecil's Ride

START

Anti-aircraft
Gun Platform

Park Place

Hong Kong Parkview

Tai Tam Reservoir Road

Wong Nai Chung
Reservoir

Take bus 6 or 66 from Exchange Square and alight on Wong Nai Chung Gap Road, just after the tennis centre and before the Hong Kong Cricket Club. A preserved set of **wartime bunkers** stands almost opposite, on either side of the petrol station.

The leftmost is known as Lawson's Bunker after **Brigadier John Lawson**, the Canadian commanding officer who died defending it. Once Kowloon had fallen to the Japanese, General Christopher Maltby organized the defenders of Hong Kong Island into two brigades. This command post was the headquarters of West Brigade, which included Lawson's Winnipeg Grenadiers as well as the Royal Scots, Punjabs and units from the Middlesex Regiment.

Brig. John Lawson

Japanese forces landed at multiple points between North Point and Shau Kei Wan on the evening of 18th December 1941, overwhelming the Indian Rajput gunners manning the coastal pillboxes, and quickly moved inland along roads and mountain trails. Hand-to-hand fighting took place around Jardine's Lookout and Mount Butler as each side lost and retook strategic hilltops. It was during this desperate time that Company **Sergeant Major John Osborn** of the Grenadiers, now remembered in a statue in Hong Kong Park, threw himself upon a grenade to save the lives of his colleagues.

Canadian soldiers arrived in Hong Kong to shore up the garrison

Wong Nai Chung Gap was a major objective for the Japanese; taking it would allow them to split the island and its defenders in two. Lawson and his unit held the position under heavy fire, with wave after wave of enemy troops mounting attacks on the bunkers. Punjabi and Royal Scots reinforcements were unable to get through. Lawson's last communication to Fortress Headquarters, on the morning of December 19th, was that he was "going outside to fight it out". He left the bunker with a pistol in each hand.

The Japanese forces admired his fighting spirit and erected a memorial to him after the war. The remaining Grenadiers held out, surrounded, for another three days before being overrun. Hong Kong's surrender came shortly afterwards, on Christmas Day.

Indian Punjabi troops

Commonwealth forces were reinforced and ready for battle

Newly arrived troops march to their camps

Singing Canadian soldier in the Toronto Star Weekly

Along with the Royal Rifles of Canada, who were deployed to the East Brigade at Tai Tam, these Winnipeg Grenadiers were the very first Canadian soldiers to see action in the Second World War. At such an early stage of the global conflict, they had received minimal training and had no combat experience. By contrast, the battle-hardened Japanese 38th Division had fought their way through China, were well equipped with heavy artillery, and had full control of the skies. The surviving Canadians became prisoners of war for the following three years and eight months of Hong Kong's occupation.

Crowded, mountainous Hong Kong must have seemed a strange place to these country boys from the faraway plains of Canada. An illustration that later appeared in the *Toronto Star Weekly* depicts a wounded Canadian soldier, singing as he marches up a street in the midst of battle. He was never seen again. Fellow soldiers sheltering in a nearby house had shouted at him to take cover. He shouted back, "It's a lovely day and it's Christmas morning."

"Who he was, where he came from and what eventually happened to him, the survivors of the Grenadiers who had shouted out to him never did learn," ran the newspaper caption. "But the unreality of this occasion – the casual, singing soldier strolling along, oblivious to the earth-shaking explosions or the hills of Hong Kong which at that moment were a mass of roaring flames – did not unduly amaze them. It was, so they thought, merely an appropriate part of the greater unreality which was the Battle of Hong Kong itself."

Cross the road again and carry on uphill, passing the **Cricket Club** – established in 1851 – on your left. The club, a mainstay of colonial life, was relocated here from Central in 1975 to make way for Chater Garden. One of the most enduring photographs from the 1960s shows cricketers in whites playing against a backdrop of Maoist posters and slogans; the old Bank of China building was used at the time as a 'shop window' for Cultural Revolution propaganda.

Central, 1967: Chairman Mao incites cricketers to revolution

Passing the **St. John's Ambulance Brigade memorial**, which pays tribute to those medics and surgeons who also lost their lives during the war, turn left up the steps and then quickly left again to follow **Sir Cecil's Ride** into the hills. This level catchwater track, named after 1920s Governor Cecil Clementi, offers occasional good views of Happy Valley and Causeway Bay. It's one of the routes that Japanese foot soldiers used to attack Wong Nai Chung Gap; they met resistance here from the Eurasian company of the Hong Kong Volunteer Defence Corps.

You may hear the gentle thwack of willow on leather as you arrive at a vantage point over the cricket club. An information board points out the location of the former Wong Nai Chung Gap Police Station, which was fought over and destroyed during the war. Its site is now occupied by the golden-gated residence of Macau casino tycoon Stanley Ho.

Low-rise Tai Hang, and a westward view of the city

Monument to fallen medical personnel

Near a pair of wooden signposts, a silver hiking sign points you uphill. These steps lead up to a covered reservoir with an open view of the valley, and then through trees to a **ruined pillbox** beside a catchwater. Detour up the steps a little higher to find a much better preserved pillbox which was used by the platoon commander of the Hong Kong Volunteers. It's hidden in woodland now, but in the 1940s the hillside was mostly bare and the pillbox would have had a sweeping view of its surroundings.

Back on the catchwater, turn left. The path ends at a closed road; bear right and you'll find yourself on top of an old anti-aircraft position. Major fighting took place here too on the morning of the 19th as the Japanese battled to capture the two guns. Down the road, the gunners' quarters are set into the hill in a more sheltered position.

Emerging onto Tai Tam Reservoir Road opposite the Parkview estate, you can cut this walk short by turning right and walking downhill to the small **Wong Nai Chung Reservoir**. It was only the third built to supply the new

Captured anti-aircraft gun

Silent sentry: pillbox still in position

city of Hong Kong, and its construction in 1899 cost the grand sum of HK$8,200. The valve house on the handsome granite dam bears the date on its lintel. It has long been superseded by far larger reservoirs in the New Territories, and is now used as a boating park. You can rent a pedalo and spend some time with turtles and carp.

Wong Nai Chung Reservoir

Below the dam, a Grade III historical building with a pitched roof is easily missed. It's still used for its original purpose of housing waterworks staff. Cross the road to take the steps back down to the bus stop on Wong Nai Chung Gap Road.

Soldier's-eye view

Otherwise, for a longer hike, turn left as you exit the wartime trail and walk past Parkview to follow Tai Tam Reservoir Road through the country park. It's an easy and enjoyable walk which crosses the Victorian-era dams, aqueducts and bridges of the four **Tai Tam reservoirs**. The park functions as a great green lung for the urban area.

Hong Kong's first reservoir at Pokfulam was only sufficient for the city's needs for twenty years; the growing population demanded more water, particularly as the idea of water closets took hold, and so the Tai Tam villagers were moved to Stanley and their valley dammed in several places. The uppermost dam was completed in 1904. Just past this, an old milestone survives to show that this was also the route of the first road, or bridle path, from Victoria (Central) to Stanley.

Byewash Reservoir valve house

Victorian civil engineering
blends into the landscape

… while in the 1960s it was in short supply

Hong Kong last saw major **water shortages** in the 1960s, when residents of some districts were limited to four hours' supply every four days, and queues at standpipes were a common sight. This led to comparatively giant reservoirs being constructed in the New Territories. In the cases of Plover Cove and High Island, they were built in former oceanic waters by blocking off bays and inlets, pumping out the seawater, and allowing the areas behind to fill with waters flowing from the surrounding mountains. Today, the annual rainy season still helps to fill Hong Kong's many reservoirs but cannot meet the needs of seven or eight million people; most water is piped in from the Dongjiang (East River) in Guangdong Province.

The track ends near the impressive granite-faced dam of the lower **Tai Tam Tuk Reservoir**. There's a foundation stone laid by Sir Henry May KCMG, the governor of the day, in 1918.

Cascading overflow from Tai Tam Tuk

Across the shallow bay, Obelisk Hill is named for the Royal Navy marker erected on it at the turn of the century as a navigational aid. This excellent defensive position, fortified with below-ground bunkers, was manned in 1941 by 'D' Company of the Royal Rifles of Canada. Its commanding officer, **Major Maurice Parker**, didn't expect his troops to be drawn into battle so quickly.

Major Maurice Parker

"The Gin Drinkers' Line had collapsed ... and we were under the impression that a large battle was being fought on the mainland," he recalled. "It turned out that fighting on the mainland was minimal, and that total casualties were very few. We were astonished to see the mainland turned over to the enemy in only five days, and judging from the casualties, without much of an attempt to stop them. We were assured that the demolitions on the mainland had been so extensive that it would take many weeks before the Japanese could bring up their artillery. The next day the first heavy shells began exploding on Hong Kong Island."

The Royal Rifles were forced back from this point to the Stanley peninsula, and fought on alongside the other Commonwealth forces until Christmas Day. After the surrender, civilians were interned at Stanley while soldiers were sent to prisoner-of-war camps in Sham Shui Po, Argyle Street and North Point.

Buses run north and south from the road, but you can make a detour directly down to sea level where, if your timing is right, you can watch overflow waters cascading down the dam's high spillway.

Quarry Bay

Formerly an area of fishing harbours, shipyards and factories, the eastern half of Hong Kong Island's northern shore has been developed since the 1980s into housing estates for the people who work in Central and other business districts. But signs of its past still remain, and it's an easy part of town to explore. This route includes pre-war relics in the country park above the city, and finishes with harbour views.

Start by jumping on any eastbound tram from Causeway Bay. The main tramway depot was located here until 1989, but Times Square now stands on the site.

A top deck seat is the best way to observe the street life of these older districts

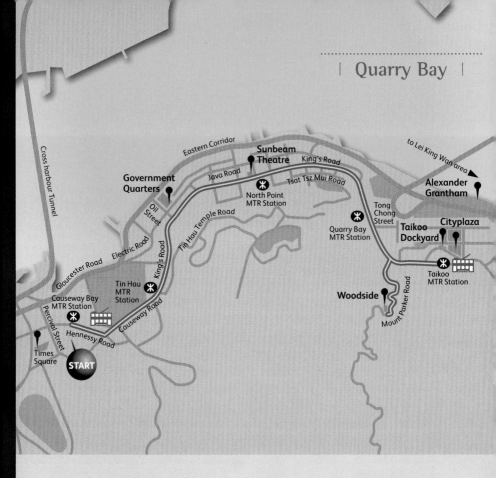

A top deck seat is the best way to observe the street life of these older districts. The **tram line** is one of the few constants in this part of Hong Kong Island; its metal tracks still trace the original route laid down in 1904. The double-deck cars retain their charming 1950s-era appearance, including some antique dials and gauges in some cases, but they are no relics: the system carries over 200,000 passengers every day.

There were teething problems when the service started. Many pedestrians couldn't grasp the concept of a vehicle with a fixed path, and would stand in its way, oblivious of the danger. Coolies discovered that pulling their carts along the tracks was much easier than on the uneven roads, and this caused major delays. In 1913, after the fall of the Qing dynasty, the company declared it would only accept Hong Kong dollars for fares, instead of the Chinese currency which had formerly also been accepted; this triggered a general anti-colonial boycott which went on for several months, the more affluent Chinese passengers taking rickshaws instead. But ridership was soon back up to normal levels. Starting in the 1960s, single-deck trailers were pulled behind the trams to carry more passengers.

Making slow progress through the North Point market

Fashion parade: trams are travelling billboards

The MTR's Island Line was tipped to replace the tramway when it opened in the 1980s, but the tram's usefulness for short journeys, and its general popularity, helped it survive. In fact it would be hard to imagine the Hong Kong streetscape without the friendly 'ding ding', as it is nicknamed in Cantonese. Over the years the trams have become travelling billboards promoting airlines, credit cards, tourist destinations, lingerie, fancy apartments, electronic gadgetry – just about everything except the tram service itself, which as the cheapest available transport doesn't need advertising. Intriguing destinations like 'Happy Valley' can bewilder the uninitiated tourist when a parade of fancy-dressed trams sashays by in slow motion, like a procession of bejewelled elephants on their lumbering way to and from some exotic festival.

Hong Kong Tramways was owned by the old trading hong Wharf Holdings, which also operates the similarly iconic Star Ferry; but the tramway was sold in 2010 to the French firm Veolia, raising hopes that this emission-free form of public transport may be in line for a renaissance.

In 1904 there were two classes of travel – first and third, rather oddly – at ten and five cents each. Today, your rattling journey along the north shore will cost HK$2, still a bargain by any measure.

Passing Fortress Hill, you can glimpse the red-brick buildings of the old Government Quarters down Oil Street. The names of Electric Road, Power Street and Tin Chong Street recall the power station which stood on the waterfront here until the 1960s.

North Point had swimming beaches until the 1920s, and seven large boulders along the shore were named the Seven Sisters, with an accompanying story of seven local maidens who pledged to remain virgins. When one of them was forced into an arranged marriage, they all drowned themselves, and were turned into stone. Tsat Tsz Mui ('Seven Sisters') Road recalls this legend. The district received a big influx of Shanghainese and Fujianese settlers after the Communist victory on the mainland in 1949, and became known in the 1950s as Little Shanghai.

The old-fashioned Sunbeam Theatre on King's Road is one of the last venues in Hong Kong to show Cantonese opera. Its lease expired in 2009, but the owner is somewhat sympathetic to this endangered local art, and with government support a permanent new venue may be found.

Relic of industry

Taikoo Docks: now Taikoo Shing

TAIKOO DOCK
COMMENCED AUGUST 1902
COMPLETED AUGUST 1907
D. MACDONALD M.I.C.E.
ENGINEER - IN - CHIEF
.I.C.E,W.G.CL

Stone survivor

Until the 1980s, Quarry Bay was the site of the vast **Taikoo Dockyard**. Built in 1902 by Butterfield & Swire, it was Hong Kong's largest at the time, and its slipways can still be traced in the modern layout of Taikoo Shing, the city's first private residential estate that now occupies part of the site. The underground car park of the Cityplaza office complex is carved out of the old graving dock. **The yard's foundation stone** still stands among the new buildings.

Taikoo is the Chinese name for Swire, and the company is still very prominent in Hong Kong business. Like HSBC, it uses for its logo an adapted version of the 'house flag' once flown from ships in the harbour. All trading hongs had different flags. The Swire flag was originally the identifier for the China Navigation Company, a shipping line which is still part of the group.

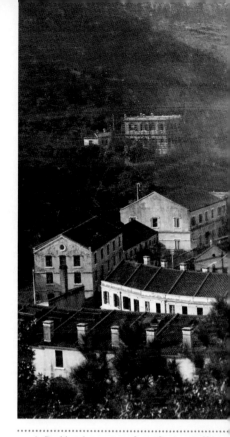

There were other industrial enterprises in the district. **Tong Chong** ('Sugar Factory') **Street**, latterly home to the South China Morning Post and the rest of the Taikoo Place office development, stands on the site of the Taikoo sugar refinery. Opening for business in the 1880s, and processing raw cane sugar brought from Java on Swire's own ships, it was the largest such facility in Asia. You can still find Taikoo-brand sugar in local shops.

Red brick quarters for refinery staff

Alight from the tram just after Tong Chong Street, opposite the 1920s-built Boys' Home. If you walk ahead to Mount Parker Road, you can make a steep ascent up the tree-shaded track to **Woodside**, an attractive red-brick mansion which was built in 1917 as staff quarters for the sugar refinery.

A scene from L.S. Lowry: Quarry Bay and the sugar factory

Right: Factory gates

During Japanese occupation, US bombers targeted the Taikoo Docks

Siege stoves, never put into service

As well as housing for the factory and dockyard workers, Swire built schools and a hospital, and a funicular railway ran from Quarry Bay to Quarry Gap, halfway up Mount Parker. No traces of these remain – the dockyard was a major bombing target during the Second World War. But you can make a detour to see some wartime ruins by carrying on up Mount Parker Road and then turning left to walk a short section of the Wilson Trail. Here on the hillside, **outdoor field stoves** were built by the government before the war in preparation for a long siege. First aid services, air raid warnings and a food rationing system were also readied. In the event, Hong Kong fell more quickly than anyone expected, and these cooking ranges were never used. Today, morning walkers have planted flowers in the spaces meant for woks.

The Wilson Trail leads back downhill towards Taikoo MTR station. Walk through the Cityplaza shopping mall, and then over the footbridge across the Eastern Corridor, to reach the other side of Quarry Bay. A harbourside park has been laid out on reclaimed land, and the retired fireboat *Alexander Grantham* is its centrepiece.

The boat was built by the Hongkong & Whampoa Dock Company in Hung Hom and entered service in 1953. It was the flagship of the Fire Services Department, participating in maritime rescues in Victoria Harbour and in the seas around Hong Kong. Perhaps its best-known firefighting action occurred in January 1972, when the *Queen Elizabeth* – a venerable ocean liner which had long been the world's largest, and which had been converted into a floating university by C.Y. Tung, shipping magnate father of Tung Chee-hwa – caught fire in the harbour. The liner capsized and eventually sank to the bottom of the harbour, where most of it still remains. Before it disappeared beneath the waves, its wreck was used as a location for the James Bond film *The Man with the Golden Gun* – a dubious honour it shared with the Tsim Sha Tsui girlie bar Bottoms Up.

Sir Alexander Grantham

The fireboat was decommissioned in 2002 and handed over to the Hong Kong Museum of History, who have converted it into an **exhibition gallery of firefighting**. Weighing in at over 500 tonnes, it required some effort to hoist it into place on land, but it's fitting that it remains beside Victoria Harbour. **Sir Alexander Grantham** himself was Governor of Hong Kong from 1947 to 1957 – a turbulent period which saw the Chinese Revolution, the Shek Kip Mei fire and rising Anglo-Chinese tensions over the Kowloon Walled City.

You can walk along the harbour to the Lei King Wan area, which has waterfront restaurants as well as the Hong Kong Film Archive, a repository of local cinema which holds regular screenings. The tram and MTR lines are within easy reach.

Blazing wreck: Seawise University in flames

Firefighting flagship

Stanley

Stanley was one of the few established settlements on Hong Kong Island when the British arrived, and was regarded as the island's unofficial capital. It was then a fishing village with perhaps a thousand inhabitants. Today, it's a popular place for expat tourists and residents, but it took more than its fair share of damage during the Second World War. This brief walking route tells the small town's story.

Sir Mark Young

Stanley's Chinese name, *Chek Chue* or 'red post', may refer to the red soil of the hillsides above it which would have been visible to the fishing crews after landslips. The British army built barracks here in the 1840s but soon found the mosquito-ridden conditions too unhealthy and decamped to the northern shore of the island. The area saw military activity again only a hundred years later, when Japanese forces landed at North Point and pushed south, and Commonwealth forces were split in two. Stanley became their final stronghold. Fierce fighting and atrocities against civilians followed until the Governor, Sir Mark Young, finally surrendered on Christmas Day 1941. Hong Kong's British, Canadian, Chinese and Indian defenders "had won indeed the lasting honour which is their due," Winston Churchill wrote later. During the years of occupation, Stanley was home to a civilian internment camp.

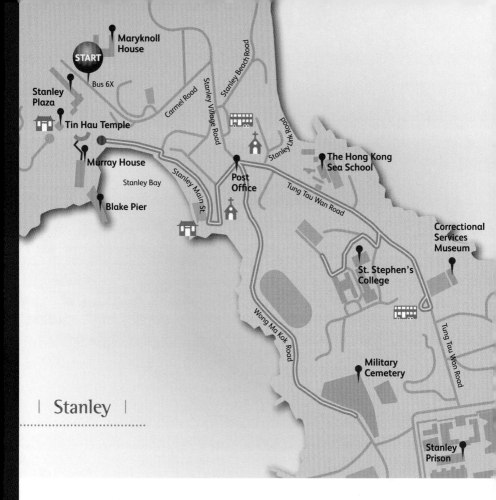

Maryknoll House

START

Bus 6X

Stanley Plaza

Tin Hau Temple

Carmel Road

Stanley Village Road

Stanley Beach Road

Stanley Link Road

Murray House

Stanley Bay

Stanley Main St.

Post Office

The Hong Kong Sea School

Tung Tau Wan Road

Blake Pier

Correctional Services Museum

St. Stephen's College

Wong Ma Kok Road

Military Cemetery

Tung Tau Wan Road

Stanley

Stanley Prison

Take bus 6X from Central, which drops you off at Stanley Plaza. Walk down through the shopping centre, built on the site of the Ma Hang squatter village, to find **Murray Building** on the waterfront.

This "magnificent quarters for the military officers" was designed by the Royal Engineers and built in Central in 1843, replacing barracks at Happy Valley which were surrounded by malarial swamp. It was used as an officers' mess. It passed from the army to the government in 1961, to become the offices of the Rating and Valuation Department, but civil servants initially refused to work there – it was reputed to be haunted following Japanese interrogations inside its walls during the war. A week-long exorcism ritual was thus carried out by monks.

Murray Building in 1970s Central...

...and in its new waterfront location

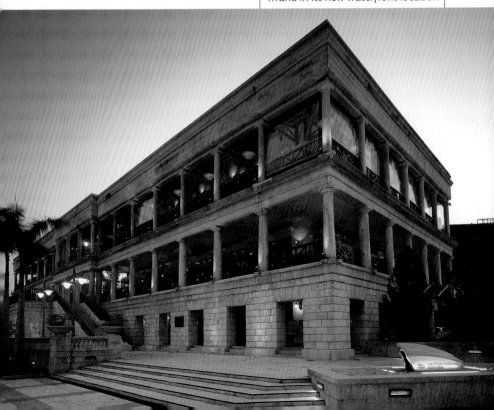

Door gods guard the patron of seafarers

Despite its status as a Grade I monument, it was demolished in 1983 to make way for the current Bank of China building. However, due to public outcry its dismantled pieces were kept in storage sheds near Tai Tam Reservoir and the building was re-erected in Stanley in 1998. The chimney-pots are not the originals; these come from the Old Mental Hospital in Sai Ying Pun.

Today it houses restaurants and bars, and the Hong Kong Maritime Museum on the ground floor tells the story of seafaring on the South China coast, from ancient trading routes and pirates to boat people and container ships. Outside, note the stone columns engraved with Chinese trading names. Like Murray Building, they were rescued from demolition in the city – in their case, from old shophouses in Shanghai Street, Kowloon. They form part of an avenue which allows Stanley's **Tin Hau temple** to keep a *feng shui* connection with the sea.

The temple displays the incense-browned pelt of a tiger which terrorized the town during the 1940s and was shot dead by a Sikh policeman. Before this, the 19th-century pirate Cheung Po-tsai was said to use the temple as a signalling station – the drum and bell would be carried outdoors to summon his vagabond brethren. The building suffered heavy damage from Typhoon Wanda in 1962 but was repaired afterwards.

Incense for Tin Hau

Shophouse pillars moved to Stanley

Blake Pier has a similar story to Murray Building. With its distinctive eaved roof, it originally stood on the praya at Central, surrounded by sampans and steamers. It was named after Sir Henry Blake, Governor from 1898 to

Henry Blake, 1898 – 1903

1903, a six-foot-three giant who had to have a special bed built for him in Government House. His time in office was a time of great change: Queen Victoria died after a reign of 64 years, the New Territories were added to the colony, and successful efforts were begun to stamp out the bubonic plague which had dogged Hong Kong's more unsanitary districts. Blake's wife threw her support behind a campaign to abolish foot-binding in China.

Blake is remembered in Blake Garden and in the *Bauhinia Blakeana* – the flower which adorns Hong Kong's modern flag and currency. The historic pier which bears his name was dismantled in 1965, moved to a bizarre inland location in Kowloon for 40 years, and re-erected at Stanley in 2007.

One distinguished visitor to arrive in Hong Kong at Blake Pier was Field Marshal Horatio Herbert Kitchener, the legendary soldier who wrested control of Sudan for the British Empire, won the Second Boer War, rose to head the Indian Army, and later – upon the outbreak of World War I – became Secretary of State for War. His image was to become iconic thanks to a much-imitated recruitment poster portraying him with an outstretched finger and the words *Your Country Needs You*. Kitchener received a hero's welcome when he landed at the pier as part of a grand tour of the colonies, and despite his handlebar moustache and civilian suit being at odds with the traditional white tunics and plumed helmets of his reception party, he took a salute from a guard of honour backed by a military band.

Rickshaw rank: Blake Pier on Connaught Road Central

Pier of the realm: a guard of honour

Relocation from the Praya to the Southside

Stamps and steamers: Blake Pier stood opposite the old GPO

Having recruited so many volunteers to the slaughter of the First World War's trenches, it was only fitting that Lord Kitchener too should die by the metaphorical sword. He drowned west of the Orkney Islands in June 1916, on a diplomatic mission to Russia, when his armoured cruiser *HMS Hampshire* struck a mine laid by a German U-boat. Most of the 655 crew perished, and Kitchener's body was never found.

Overlooking Stanley Bay, and clearly visible if you arrive by bus, **Maryknoll House** is a Chinese-themed construction of red-brick walls and green glazed roof tiles. It was built in 1935 as the headquarters of the Maryknoll Mission, and housed a language school for Catholic priests on their way to various parts of southern China. A space under the main entrance was used as a

The Maryknoll Fathers

A restful location above the town

waiting room for rickshaw boys and sedan chair porters. Stanley was chosen for its location over other peaceful sites at Tuen Mun and Sai Kung, as the former was then malarial and the latter had no road access.

"I presume that you understand just what a rest house is," wrote Father Patrick Byrne to a benefactor in 1930, "But in case you may not, I might explain that it is the custom for our missioners to spend several months either in one particular station in the Interior, or visiting various stations, and after months of this, including as it does today more or less precarious travel because of bandits and Bolshevists, as well as poor food and all sorts of delightful company like fleas and such – a vacation of a couple of weeks at the rest house looks more or less like a million dollars. These periods mean much towards maintaining the morale of the men."

Mission mansion: Maryknoll House today

"We have good ventilation and light, and the nights are quiet with only the washing of waves on the shore below, or the call of a fisherman out in the bay," reported one of the priests. "There are none of the cat and dog symphonies [of Kowloon] and the motor road is too far away to cause any disturbance." Perhaps it was altogether too agreeable for those accustomed to more ascetic conditions: a visiting archbishop said in 1937, "You will have to stay a long time in Purgatory because of the comfort you have here."

The house was commandeered by the Japanese secret police during the war. Upon their surrender in 1945, nuns from the Carmelite convent down the road briefly moved in, to prevent doors and floorboards being looted for firewood. Shortly afterwards, the house became a refuge for missionaries thrown out of China after the Communist victory of 1949. Hospitality must have been second to none – one priest exiting China, Father Anthony Maloney, apparently came to Maryknoll for dinner and stayed for eight years.

'Tables 88' restaurant

Beyond the crowded, narrow lanes of Stanley Market, Hong Kong's oldest surviving **police station** stands on Stanley Village Road. For many years occupied by a restaurant, and now by a supermarket, it was built in 1859 and also served as the harbour master's office. The building was the scene of the final hand-to-hand fighting in 1941.

The town's **postage-stamp-sized post office** is next door. It was built in 1937 and was restored in 2007 for its 70th anniversary. It's the oldest still in use. An antique stamp issuing machine is set into the outer wall, and the postbox and one of the windows are engraved with 'GR' (King George VI) insignia. Inside, it has been beautifully restored to its 1930s appearance, modern tiles having been removed to expose the original terrazzo flooring beneath.

The Hong Kong Sea School on Tung Tau Wan Road, a training school for sea cadets, was opened by King Baudouin of Belgium in 1964. Further on, the gates of Stanley Prison bar the road. The jail was built in 1937 to house the colony's high-security prisoners; at the time, Stanley was considered a remote place suitable for exiling hardened criminals. Hong Kong's last hanging took place here in 1966. The compound contains a mosque, a reminder that the prison service, like the police force, was originally staffed largely by Indians.

Sea urchins: the cadet school

Royal Mail: cyphers of postboxes now disappearing

You can't enter the prison (unless you've been sent there) but you can step inside the Hong Kong **Correctional Services Museum**, which is right next door. Galleries detail the development of Hong Kong's penal system since colonial times. Exhibits like the Victorian flogging rack may strengthen your resolve to be a law-abiding citizen. There's a mock cell for death row inmates, and a description of the sequence of events leading up to the gallows – the hangman would spend the evening testing different weights on the rope, a process clearly audible to the condemned man. A Dickens-style log book records, in flowing script, the lesser punishments dished out to unruly prisoners. Other galleries trace the more recent history of the Vietnamese boat people in Hong Kong, who were held in camps, and display some of the handicrafts made by inmates.

Detained at Her Majesty's pleasure

The prison service – a cosmopolitan crew

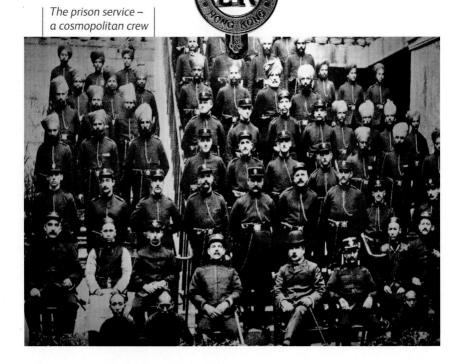

Public punishments were commonplace

The museum details the measures meted out to miscreants

Floating population:
Vietnamese boat people
arrived on overcrowded
fishing vessels

St. Stephen's Chapel contains military memorials

The prison mosque, place of worship for Islamic officers

Great and good: the college founders

Opposite the museum, the bungalows and playing fields of **St. Stephen's College** occupy a hill above the road. St. Stephen's was founded by a group of businessmen including Ho Kai, of Kai Tak airport fame, in 1903 as an English school for Chinese children. It was moved to these spacious Stanley grounds in the 1930s and attracted Chinese students from all over Southeast Asia. A massacre of medical staff and wounded soldiers took place here on the day of surrender in 1941, and the college, along with parts of the neighbouring prison, was turned into an internment camp for Allied civilians.

The three years and eight months of captivity saw overcrowding and deprivation, with over two thousand people – mostly women and children – crammed into the camp. Food and medicines were smuggled in by operatives working undercover with the British Army Aid Group, but nevertheless many detainees died. The camp was hit by an American bomb in the later stages of the war, causing further loss of life. Finally, after the British fleet had sailed back into Victoria Harbour in August 1945, the Union Jack was once more hoisted at Stanley – in the prison grounds – to scenes of joy and relief.

Liberation day: the Union Flag is raised once more in the internment camp

The **military cemetery** can be found by following Wong Ma Kok Road (or by walking through the college grounds). Cared for by the Commonwealth War Graves Commission, the cemetery is a quiet spot often used for picnics or studying. Up the steps from the war memorial, there are three types of graves. Many date from the earliest days of colonial Hong Kong, and record those who were killed in skirmishes with pirates, and those who died from tropical diseases. Two young soldiers were ambushed by pirates – possibly from the nearby village – while transporting their regiment's pay by boat from Victoria in 1844. The uniform white stones mark the graves of those who died in the defence of Hong Kong in 1941, and the rough-hewn granite stones mark those who died in the internment camp later on. A separate monument to the *Francais Libres* remembers the Free French who joined the locally raised volunteer corps and died during the conflict.

The road ends at Stanley Fort, an army base which occupies the whole southern portion of the peninsula. It was laid out in 1937 in the run-up to war, displacing the residents of Wong Ma Kok village who were moved to new houses in Stanley. These eight brick homes, built by the British Army in Chinese village style and now known as Pat Kan Uk, still stand on the southern edge of Stanley market.

Rough-hewn stones mark the victims of war

Remembering those who gave their lives for Hong Kong

Cheung Chau

The tiny fishing isle of Cheung Chau has a long history and is home to more people than all Hong Kong's other outlying islands combined. Popular hikes take in the rocky bays and so-called 'pirate cave' of its southern coast, but you can make a different circuit of its cheek-by-jowl central area, where people have lived for centuries and lots of built heritage has survived.

Take any ferry from Pier 5 in Central. Arriving on Cheung Chau less than an hour later, turn right and make your way along the praya, past the seating of outdoor restaurants and the municipal market building. Bicycles tied to waterfront railings are matched by sampans moored on the other side. The word 'sampan' means 'three planks', a reference to the small boat's simple but long-lived design.

...which carries on to the present day

The island has a long fishing history...

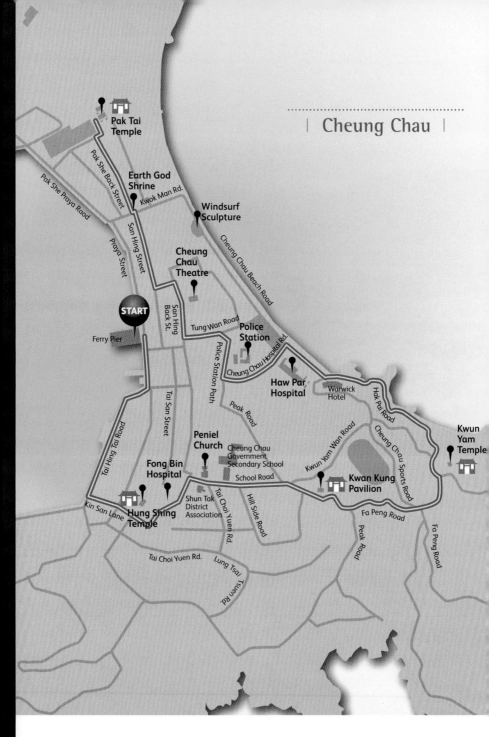

Pak Tai
Temple

Pak She Praya Raod

Pak She Back Street

Earth God
Shrine

Kwok Man Rd.

Windsurf
Sculpture

San Hing Street

Cheung Chau Beach Road

Cheung
Chau
Theatre

Praya Street

START

San Hing
Back St.

Tung Wan Road

Police
Station

Cheung Chau Hospital Rd.

Ferry Pier

Police Station Path

Haw Par
Hospital

Warwick
Hotel

Hak Pai Road

Cheung Chau Sports Road

Kwun
Yam
Temple

Tai San Street

Peak Road

Peniel
Church

Cheung Chau
Government
Secondary School

Kwun Yam Wan Road

Tai Hing Tai Road

Fong Bin
Hospital

School Road

Kwan Kung
Pavilion

Kin San Lane

Hung Shing
Temple

Shun Tak
District
Association

Tai Choi Yuen Rd.

Hill Side Road

Fa Peng Road

Peak Road

Fa Peng Road

Tai Choi Yuen Rd.

Lung Tsai

Tsuen Rd.

| Cheung Chau |

Turn left into a shaded plaza occupied by restaurant tables. At the far end of the square, you can see the **Hung Shing temple** perched on a rise and half-hidden by shopfronts. Reach it by taking steps up beside a stonemason's workshop and turning left at the old street sign made rusty by salty sea air. Like Tin Hau, Hung Shing is a deity of seafarers, and this beautifully maintained temple to him was built in 1813.

Qing-dynasty temple to a seafaring god

| Crumbling hospital gateway |

Backstreet banyan: outspread branches offer shade

Leaving by the other end of the temple compound, a jumble of potted plants, clothes lines and delivery trolleys leads to the gate of the crumbling **Fong Bin** ('Convenient') **Hospital**. Funded by charitable donations and supported by Lai Chun-bin, a high-ranking official of the Qing navy, it was established in the 1870s, twenty years before Cheung Chau passed into British hands as part of the New Territories. Without much in the way of medical facilities apart from a dispensary of Chinese medicine, it operated more as a hospice for the local poor and as a mortuary for those drowned in nearby shipwrecks. It was renovated in 1951 but abandoned by 1988.

Despite its current ruinous state, the pioneering hospital has been accorded Grade III heritage status and may be renovated in the future. An outbuilding on the slope beside it is dated the 36th year of the Chinese Republic; this calendar system began in 1911 with the overthrow of the Qing dynasty, and so corresponds to 1947.

The busier building behind the hospital houses the local Shun Tak District Association. Many Hong Kong people trace their ancestry to towns in other parts of the Pearl River Delta such as Shun Tak, Sze Yap or Toi Shan. Follow the path downhill to leave the compound by another archway, then turn right and pass the whitewashed ramparts of **Peniel Church** to reach School Road. Note the colonial postbox, originally red but painted green since the handover, with its 'GR' (King George V) crest.

Take the steps uphill. The Cheung Chau Government Secondary School, known until the 1960s as the Anglo-Chinese School, was used by the Japanese as their headquarters on the island during the Second World War.

| Taoist pavilion |

| Granite cornerstone |

| Colonial relic, formerly red |

At the top of the steps, pass through iron gates to enter the well-kept gardens of the **Kwan Kung Pavilion**. It's not old, having been built only in 1973, but keeps to a traditional Taoist style. It is dedicated to Kwan Ti, the red-faced god of war and righteousness whose image is often seen in shrines at the back of shops and restaurants. Intriguingly, he is venerated by both police officers and triads. A two-metre long 'dragon bone' is on display in a glass case – it was found in the nets of local fishermen.

Verdant villas: sprawling residences on Peak Road

Gate to Kwun Yam's seaside temple

觀音古廟

Returning to the gates, turn left onto Peak Road. Access to this area was once restricted to Europeans in an effort to develop an exclusive residential district like The Peak on Hong Kong Island. Houses up here are noticeably grander and more individual in style: one garden wall is decorated with gryphon motifs, for instance.

Downhill, you'll find the island's small **Kwun Yam temple** overlooking the sea. The beach below it is named for the temple's goddess of mercy, although it is also called Afternoon Beach by resident expats who follow the sun's rays around from Morning Beach.

Sporting monument　　　*Cheung Chau's Olympian*

Take the coastal path left from here. The café on the little headland is run by relatives of **Lee Lai-shan**, the Cheung Chau windsurfer who became Hong Kong's first-ever Olympic gold medal winner, at the 1996 Games in Atlanta. In a sense she was also the last, since one year later, the Hong Kong team was obliged to add 'China' to its name. Lee has since retired from competition and married another local windsurfing champion. She was the first torch-bearer during Hong Kong's Olympic flame relay leg in 2008.

Tropical verandahs of the island's hospital...

Below the Warwick Hotel, an ancient rock carving is protected by a perspex screen. Its purpose and age are unknown, though it is thought to date back 3,000 years, and may have been intended to protect fishermen while out at sea. In those times, Hong Kong was inhabited by the aboriginal Yuet people.

Ahead stands the **Haw Par Hospital**, run by the St. John Ambulance Association. Walk around its perimeter to reach the entrance. It's a beautiful building of colonnaded verandahs dating from the 1930s. There is a bust of its founder Aw Boon Haw in the lobby, and it's worth reading the inscription recorded on behalf of the grateful islanders.

Born in Rangoon in 1882, the Burmese-Chinese tycoon Aw Boon Haw made his fortune from the manufacture of the famous Tiger Balm ointment. ('Boon Haw' means 'gentle tiger' in his native Hakka tongue.) He was a great philanthropist and built the Tiger Balm Gardens in Hong Kong and Singapore, which were free for the public to enter, as well as funding hospitals and schools across China. He also founded several Southeast Asian newspapers including *Sing Tao and The Standard* – originally named the *Hong Kong Tiger Standard*. For a while, he drove a custom-made car with a sculpted tiger's head on the bonnet. Boon Haw's brother and business partner was called Boon Par ('gentle leopard'), and so the Haw Par Hospital commemorates them both.

As you leave, turn left uphill and then bear right. A small cannon symbolically guards the island's **police station**, a little-known colonial building dating from 1913. It was built in response to the murder of three Indian police constables by a band of pirates in August 1912.

Going downhill again, make a left turn onto Tung Wan Road, lined with cafés and bars and busy with foot traffic between the pier and the beach. The road opens onto a square dominated at the far corner by a venerable banyan. In the 1990s, a proposal was made to fell this tree to improve passage for Cheung Chau's tiny fire engines. Rather than allow this to happen, the low-rise market buildings around it were demolished instead.

… and its peaceful police station

長洲戲院

The curtain has fallen on the Cheung Chau Theatre

Don't walk as far as the tree; instead, turn right immediately upon entering the square to follow San Hing Back Street a short distance. Here on the right stands the deserted but evocative **Cheung Chau Theatre**, built in 1931. In its earliest days it showed silent films, with interpreters at hand to narrate the plot to the audience. It continued showing Chinese and Western films throughout the heyday of Cantonese cinema until it was finally closed in the early 1990s. Its last cinematic act was to serve as the shooting location for the nostalgic local movie *Just One Look* in 2001.

You can peek through the theatre's shutters to see into the lobby. The building is a rare survivor of its era, and with any luck will be preserved and put to good use along the lines of the similar Yaumatei Theatre.

Girls on film: Cantonese cinema reflected the changes in Hong Kong's evolving society

Sail and steam take shelter in the island's enveloping harbour

The next left-then-right puts you on San Hing Street. Shops on either side of this narrow alley sell almost everything an islander might need. Traditional trades like herbalists, incense sellers and chandlers (ships' outfitters) survive among the bakeries, fashion boutiques and dessert shops. At the crossroads with Kwok Man Road, there is an **earth god shrine**. Go straight ahead onto Pak She Street. Further along, on the right, the hall of a local clan association is open to the street. Faded photos on the wall show Cheung Chau as it was in 1927 and 1953.

The street opens onto the forecourt of the **Pak Tai temple**, the island's most famous, alternatively known as Yuk Hui Kung – 'Palace of the Jade Void'. It is devoted to the God of the North, a mysterious Taoist deity also known as the Supreme Emperor of Dark Heaven. It's here that the annual bun festival is held, with a procession of costumed local children invisibly balanced on floats, and towers made of steamed buns. For at least three days, the island is packed with tourists, and all residents and visitors are expected to abstain from eating meat.

Crowds gather for the festival parade

Costumed children

Pak Tai temple
welcomes worshippers

Banners and buns: the island's busiest time

The temple was built in 1783 following an outbreak of plague on Cheung Chau which was banished when an image of Pak Tai was brought to the island. Among the usual antique drums and bells inside, you'll find an iron sword dating from the Song dynasty and a Qing-era sedan chair which are carried on parade with the Pak Tai statue during the **bun festival**. A golden crown for the statue was presented by a local worshipper to mark the visit of Britain's Princess Margaret in 1966.

Basketball courts show your way to the harbour, busy with craft of all sizes. Turn left onto the praya which is lined with open-air restaurants. Treat yourself to a few dishes of seafood and a bucket of cold beers, and take your time over it – the ferry pier is just five minutes further along the waterfront.

Tsim Sha Tsui

Tsim Sha Tsui – 'narrow sandspit', after its original pointed shape – was added to the territory of Hong Kong in 1860 along with the rest of Kowloon as far north as today's Boundary Street. This followed the brief but bloody Arrow War, the same conflict that saw British and French troops burn the Summer Palace in Peking. Today, the archaic spelling of the district's name confuses the tourists who stay at hotels here. Pronounced something approximating *Jeem Sah Joy* in Cantonese, many foreign residents prefer to call it Chimsy or simply TST. This walking route takes in most of the area's historic attractions.

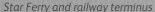

Star Ferry and railway terminus

Today's TST after a century and a half of reclamation

Vessels of all sizes ply the deep harbour

The acquisition of the Kowloon peninsula and the adjacent Stonecutters Island added a little over three square miles to the colony's land area, but more importantly allowed easier defence of the harbour. Batteries, barracks and docks were quickly built on the new addition.

It's best to arrive by **Star Ferry**. (Both the Central and Wanchai piers run services to Tsim Sha Tsui). The familiar green vessels have been crossing the harbour from here since the late 1800s, their double-ended design saving time departing from each side. The service was started in its current form by Dorabjee Naorojee, a Parsee businessman who regularly ferried friends and family over to Kowloon and decided to start charging for the trip. Over a century later, the journey is still a bargain.

Hong Kong owes its early business success to the deep waters of Victoria Harbour – all sizes of ships could call here. Besides naval and merchant vessels, cruise liners began serving the city. Mail also arrived by steamer. With the unloading of goods and the embarkation of passengers, the waterfront was a constant hive of activity. The long berths of **Ocean Terminal** were opened in 1966 on the site of the old Kowloon wharves, and the first ocean-going liner to dock here was the P&O vessel **Canberra**. The landlord of Ocean Terminal and Harbour City is still known as Wharf – having shortened its name from the

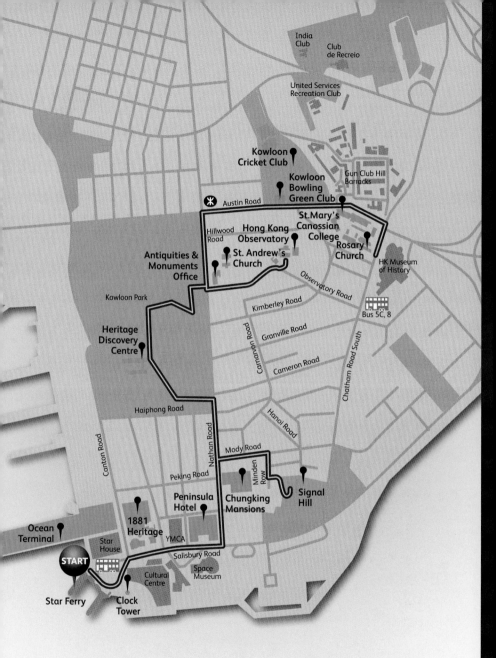

Kowloon
Cricket Club

Kowloon
Bowling
Green Club

Gun Club Hill
Barracks

Austin Road

St.Mary's
Canossian
College

Hillwood
Road

Hong Kong
Observatory

St. Andrew's
Church

Rosary
Church

Antiquities &
Monuments
Office

HK Museum
of History

Kowloon Park

Observatory Road

Kimberley Road

Bus 5C, 8

Heritage
Discovery
Centre

Cameron Road

Granville Road

Cameron Road

Chatham Road South

Haiphong Road

Hanoi Road

Nathan Road

Mody Road

Canton Road

Peking Road

Minden Row

Signal
Hill

Peninsula
Hotel

Chungking
Mansions

Ocean
Terminal

1881
Heritage

YMCA

Star
House

Salisbury Road

Space
Museum

START

Star Ferry

Clock
Tower

Cultural
Centre

India
Club

Club
de Recreio

United Services
Recreation Club

Tsim Sha Tsui

The Heiyo Maru dominates the busy wharf in this 1930s scene

In 1997, Ocean Terminal simultaneously hosted the Queen Elizabeth II and the Canberra

Kowloon Wharf and Godown Company in the 1980s – and this firm also operates the Star Ferry. One of the five flagpoles beside the terminal flies the traditional Wharf 'house flag' which once identified its ships in the harbour.

Turning right upon exiting the ferry pier brings you to the free-standing **clock tower** which was part of the old Kowloon-Canton Railway terminus. The steam-powered railway was inaugurated in 1910 as part of a scheme to link Hong Kong to London by rail via the Trans-Siberian route. This halved the time needed to make the journey – ships took six weeks – but most colonial types still opted for the sea voyage. The terminus was a grand and well loved landmark of Hong Kong, but was demolished to widespread dismay in 1975 and a new station built in Hung Hom. The **Cultural Centre** and **Space Museum** were built over the former tracks. Apart from the clock tower, six of the station's granite columns survive in a park in Tsim Sha Tsui East.

Sir Matthew Nathan

Sir Matthew Nathan was made governor in 1904 partly to expedite the ambitious railway project. As a former army engineer rather than diplomat, he had the necessary experience to meet the challenges

The KCR terminus and clock tower decked out for Queen Elizabeth's 1953 coronation

of tunnelling under Lion Rock to extend the line into the newly-leased New Territories. He took a personal interest in the survey work along the route. But there were other difficulties: the Viceroy of Canton had no funds available to complete the Chinese section, and conflicting concessions had been awarded

Nathan's Folly: ahead of its time

to other parties, among them the Americans and the French. Nathan solved these problems by loaning the Chinese authorities over a million pounds sterling. Through services to Canton began in October 1911 – just in time for Sun Yat-sen's revolution which deposed the Viceroy along with the Emperor.

Nathan also widened the road that today bears his name. Prior to this, it was known as Robinson Road after Sir William Robinson, the governor in office at the time of Kowloon's addition to the colony. (Robinson Road in the Mid-Levels is named after Sir Hercules Robinson, a different, and evidently more popular, governor). Further north, part of the road was known as Coronation Road after King Edward VII, successor to Queen Victoria. Critics dubbed the newly widened road **'Nathan's Folly'** – at the time, motor cars were a rare sight in Hong Kong and such a wide avenue seemed an extravagance.

Being Jewish and unmarried – two traits unique in Hong Kong's governors – Nathan was not without his detractors, but his time in office was successful and he went on to become Governor of Queensland.

Falun Gong practitioners hold an almost permanent protest near the clock tower, displaying photographs of alleged atrocities against their number by the Chinese government. While the post-handover 'one country, two systems' arrangements are still in place, they remain free to do so.

The innocuous **bus terminus** is currently the subject of a campaign to save it from redevelopment; apparently it has been in operation since the 1920s and is a place of collective memory. This is probably less a reflection of its intrinsic worth as a heritage site than an indication that we have little tangible heritage left,

Buses and boats in the 20s

and what we have is often badly mismanaged. A case in point exists just over the street.

Cross Salisbury Road towards **Star House**. Here on the opposite corner, a new hotel and shopping complex called **Heritage 1881** occupies the site of the old Marine Police Headquarters. The police moved out in 1994, and for many years the leafy Victorian compound lay empty while possible uses for it were discussed. Few people expected the eventual result that 2009 revealed.

The former Marine Police Headquarters

Before development, the grounds boasted Hong Kong's only mature date palm

When I first saw what had been done, my breath was literally taken away. Not only had most of the century-old trees been chopped down, but the very hill that the police station stood on had been excavated to allow yet another shopping mall and plaza to be inserted beneath it – in an area which is hardly short of vacuous watch and fashion shops. The effect is that of a modern casino or theme park. By removing the hill which allowed the Marine Police to watch over the harbour, the developer has destroyed the historical context of the site, but it is the government which is responsible for allowing this act of vandalism. Of course preservation is better than demolition; but this site represents an incredible wasted opportunity, and it's hard to understand how our bureaucrats can keep getting it so badly wrong.

The original police station, a graceful colonnaded building dating from 1884, has been converted into the Hullett House hotel. Parts of it are open to the public. Go up to hotel level and you can walk through to the courtyard, the walls of which hold bird boxes for the pigeons which once carried messages to ships in the harbour. The Mariners' Rest bar occupies the former police sergeants' mess, and dozens of old photographs line the walls. You can have a drink in the holding cells. Outside, a grill restaurant is housed in the former stables.

Originally called the Water Police, the **Marine Police** commenced operations as soon as the colony was founded in 1841. With waters overrun by pirates and smugglers, and a large population of boat people, they had a full plate from day one. They were housed in a ship moored in the harbour until this headquarters was built for them on a promontory which, before reclamation, had clear views out to sea on three sides. In 1941, the Japanese occupied the building and shelled Hong Kong Island from its now-vanished front lawn; they then used it as their naval headquarters for the duration of the war. The Marine Police kept the admiral's swivel chair, and a Japanese flag, as mementoes.

On the corner of the compound overlooking Canton Road, the circular white tower known as the **Round House** was the home of Hong Kong's first time ball. Every day at 1:00 pm, a large copper ball was lowered from the mast atop the tower. This allowed ships in the harbour to correct their timekeeping

Former noonday gun?

equipment. Another tall mast was used to display typhoon signals. The time ball was in operation until 1907, when its view of the harbour was partially blocked by new buildings and it was moved to a higher site at Signal Hill a little further east.

Other relics on site include gas-fired lampposts and a three-pound Hotchkiss gun. This may be the cannon which was swapped in 1961 with the Noonday Gun fired daily by Jardines in Causeway Bay, after noise complaints from local residents; but so much mythology surrounds the Noonday Gun, it's hard to be sure.

Return to the Salisbury Road entrance and turn left. The two-storey brick building which is now a Shanghai Tang outlet was built as TST's first fire station in 1920. After 1971 it was used for many years by a local arts and culture association. Before you enter the underpass, squeeze through the gap at the side of the building: an antique Dennis fire engine has been preserved and is on display.

Walk around the **YMCA** to reach the **Peninsula Hotel**, familiarly known as the Pen, which opened its doors in 1928 and retains its elegant, old-world charm. It's still operated by its founders, the long-resident Kadoorie family. The lobby is a popular place for afternoon tea – expect to wait for a table at weekends.

The Peninsula was conceived as a railway hotel to take advantage of business from the new station just across the road. The 'roaring twenties' were in full swing – it was a time of liberalism, prosperity, art deco and modern-minded 'flapper' girls – and travel by train and ocean liner was becoming accessible to those of moderate means. The Pen quickly became an important part of Hong Kong's social world.

It was here – in Room 336, to be precise – on Christmas evening 1941 that the governor, Sir Mark Young, signed the surrender documents in the presence of Japanese Lieutenant-General Takashi Sakai. The candlelit ceremony was difficult to capture on camera, and so an artist was commissioned to record the scene. For the duration of the war, the hotel was renamed the Toa, or 'East Asia'.

The Peninsula is famous for its fleet of Rolls-Royces, but since a new tower with a landing pad was added in 1995, guests have the added option of arriving by helicopter.

Venerable venues: the YMCA and the Peninsula, then and now

Railway hotel: the Peninsula

Chungking Mansions: an earlier incarnation

Exiting and joining Nathan Road, turn left. This rather overpowering stretch of hotels, restaurants, shops and tireless touts is known as the 'Golden Mile' and forms many tourists' first impressions of Hong Kong. Stop at Peking Road and look across at the daunting bulk of **Chungking Mansions**. A high-class apartment block when it was built in the 1960s, it has for many years been a warren of cheap guesthouses, workshops, grocery stores and curry houses with the most cosmopolitan mix of people in Hong Kong. The building has a reputation for crime which isn't really warranted, and a small measure of cinematic fame thanks to Wong Kar-wai's *Chungking Express*. As well as a haven for budget-minded backpackers, it's an important staging post on the small-scale trade routes between China, South Asia and Africa.

Enter the ground-floor arcade of Chungking Mansions. Small shops serve foods and sell items imported from all over the developing world. If you aim

Elegant lobby of the 30s

Sir Mark Young's surrender

for the back of the arcade and bear left, you'll find a grimy alley – typical of Tsim Sha Tsui – which leads out onto Minden Row.

Here on your right, a track winds up **Signal Hill** to a quiet garden which contains Hong Kong's second **time ball tower**. This one is taller than the earlier example, in order to be more visible from the harbour. It was built in 1907 in Edwardian style and remained in use until 1933, when radio and telephones rendered the time ball service obsolete. After some decades of neglect, during which it was used as an ammunition store, it was restored and opened to the public in 1980. There's a good view from the top.

Time ball tower

Signal Hill

Heritage in the park

Kowloon British School

Returning via Mody Road to Nathan Road, walk north through the crowds to find the busy entrance to Kowloon Park. This large green lung was the site of Whitfield Barracks from the 1890s until the 1960s, and some of its large old trees date from its army days; it now offers a welcome breathing space for this crowded district. The mosque beside the entrance was originally built for Indian soldiers in the British Army.

Four of the old barrack buildings have been retained. Two of them housed Hong Kong's Museum of History for 15 years. Now, they have been converted into the **Heritage Discovery Centre**, with an exhibition of local sites which have received conservation awards from UNESCO. There are other military relics in the park: a former gun position on the western side is now a lookout point, a battery which predates the barracks is now the children's discovery playground, and there are several closed entrances to air-raid shelters.

Following the walkway over the outdoor swimming pools points you back towards Nathan Road, and almost directly opposite stand the red-brick premises of the **Antiquities and Monuments Office**. This government body occupies the former Kowloon British School, built in 1902 with a donation from Jardines compradore Sir Robert Ho Tung. Ho Tung was a Eurasian who battled the prejudices of his day to become the first non-European to be

Weather station: the once-Royal Observatory

granted permission to live on the Peak. His skill at business – a compradore was an intermediary who struck deals between Western and Chinese merchants – made him Hong Kong's richest man, and he was generous with his wealth.

The students later moved to a larger building in Ho Man Tin and the school was renamed King George V, known in shorthand today as KGV. It's the oldest school in the ESF system. For some years this original building was the home of the Tsim Sha Tsui 'kaifong' or neighbourhood welfare association. You can't wander around inside, but free guided tours are offered every Friday afternoon.

On the hill behind it, once marked on maps as Mount Elgin, the **Hong Kong Observatory** is hidden in its own little reserve of tropical forest. Built in 1883, around the same time as the Marine Police Headquarters, it's a beautiful building with long verandahs. Meteorologists have been issuing weather reports, typhoon signals and warnings to shipping from here for over 120 years. The Observatory was awarded the 'Royal' prefix in 1912 by King George V but dropped it in 1997. Guided tours of the compound are given, in Cantonese only, on two or three Saturdays every month.

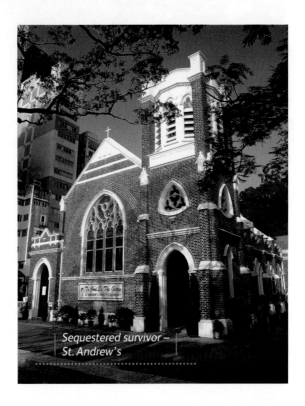

*Sequestered survivor –
St. Andrew's*

Next door to the Antiquities and Monuments Office, **St. Andrew's Church** is another century-old survivor. It sits in peaceful grounds which are a surprise to find in such a busy part of Kowloon. It's an Anglican church which was built with funds donated by Sir Catchick Paul Chater, the founder of the Kowloon Wharf and Godown Company, in 1906. Chater had a house and garden next door which covered the area now occupied by Hillwood Road. In those days, Kowloon was mostly suburban, and beyond Austin Road there was little but fields.

Bishop Joseph Hoare, who laid the foundation stone of the church, didn't live to see its opening; he was drowned, along with thousands of others, in the great typhoon of 18th September 1906. The same storm destroyed the Star Ferry pier, sank over two thousand ships and beached the steamer *Fat Shan* on Gascoigne Road. The disaster prompted the government to build breakwaters and typhoon shelters.

The attractive vicarage next to the church was built in 1909. Its first occupant, Reverend Hubert Spink, founded Hong Kong's first scout troop. St. Andrew's bell tower was restored for the church's centenary in 2006.

Governor on the green: Sir Geoffrey Northcote

Just north of here, you can break this walk in two by finishing at Jordan MTR station. Otherwise, turn right onto Austin Road and walk along to the **Kowloon Bowling Green Club**.

The club was founded in 1900 by a group of Scotsmen who enjoyed playing lawn bowls near their homes on Knutsford Terrace. The first wooden clubhouse was opened on the current premises in 1905. Sir Matthew Nathan did the honours, and apparently left on horseback for Tai Po directly afterwards, no doubt to check on the progress of the Kowloon-Canton Railway tracks.

Behind it, the **Kowloon Cricket Club** occupies an adjoining green. No colonial society was complete without a cricket ground. League cricket was established in Hong Kong in 1903, with teams including the Hong Kong Cricket Club, Parsee Cricket Club, Royal Engineers, Craigengower Cricket Club, Army Ordinance Corps, Civil Service and HMS Tamar competing for the South China Morning Post Shield. The KCC was established the following year, and its first clubhouse was opened by Hormusjee Mody in 1908. The current white-stucco building dates from 1932.

During the war years, the greens of both clubs were dug up and used as vegetable gardens. Other long-established clubs in the neighbourhood include the United Services Recreation Club, which has military origins and still leases army land; the Club de Recreio, founded by the once-large Portuguese community; and the India Club.

Further down Austin Road, Gun Club Hill Barracks occupy the hill overlooking Chatham Road. These were transferred to the People's Liberation Army in 1997, but the Chinese garrison in Hong Kong is much smaller than the British number ever was, so it's unlikely you'll see anyone around.

The long gallery of St. Mary's faces the Museum of History

St. Mary's Canossian College on the opposite corner is one of the city's most prestigious girls' schools. It was founded by the Roman Catholic Canossian Daughters of Charity in 1900 and was originally intended for local Portuguese girls. The Old Building, facing Chatham Road, was built in 1925 in neo-classical style, while the upper Main Building dates from 1930. Today its student body is mostly Chinese. Alumnae include several local actresses and politicians.

The colourful Rosary Church next door was also built primarily for the Portuguese residents of the area, but its earliest congregation also included British soldiers, Goans, Spanish from Manila and local Indians. Built in 1905 and dedicated to Our Lady of Pompeii, Queen of the Rosary, it's the oldest Catholic church in Kowloon. Having an Italian parish priest in 1941 meant that it was left alone by the Japanese forces and functioned normally throughout the occupation.

This walk ends at the purpose-built Hong Kong Museum of History across the road, which has ample space to do justice to its permanent exhibition, 'The Hong Kong Story'. It's well recommended for anyone new to town or new to Hong Kong's heritage. Buses 5C and 8 travel down Chatham Road back to the Star Ferry.

Hung Hom and the Harbour Ferries

In the days before the MTR and cross-harbour tunnels, many points around Victoria Harbour were linked by a network of ferry routes. Some of them still operate, and riding them offers a different perspective on our familiar impressions of the city. This walk takes you around the little-touristed Kowloon districts of Hung Hom and To Kwa Wan.

From the North Point ferry pier, take the ferry across to Hung Hom. It's just $5.50 for the 10-minute crossing. Alternatively, take bus 7B from Lok Fu MTR, or a brief taxi ride from TST. The useful Star Ferry service from Central and Wan Chai ceased in 2011, but the destination has long links with the seafaring trade.

From junks to aircraft carriers, the harbour was Hong Kong's highway

Beached: a shopping mall ashore in Hung Hom

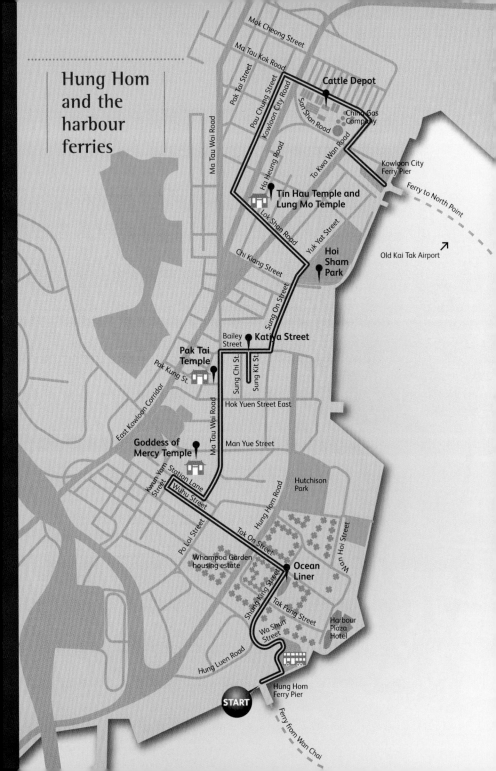

At Hung Hom, the promenade is popular with anglers who hopefully don't eat the harbour fish they catch. The tall blue glass tower is the Harbour Plaza Hotel, where Chinese President Jiang Zemin stayed during the handover ceremonies in 1997. This was the first visit to Hong Kong by a Chinese head of state for over 700 years; the only previous known visit was by the two Sung princes in 1277, and they were on the run from the Mongols.

Cross the bus terminus to find a passage into the Whampoa Garden housing estate. You might be surprised to see an **ocean liner** jammed between the apartment blocks. In fact it's a mere concrete shell for a Japanese department store and wouldn't float, but its presence recalls the mighty dockyards which once dominated this part of town.

Dry dock: Whampoa's heritage

Long funnelled ferry for a 1930s crossing

The dockyard serviced ships of all flags

The Hongkong & Whampoa Dock Company was established in 1863, soon after Kowloon fell into British hands, to supplement the dockyards already repairing vessels at Aberdeen. It was named after a yard formerly used at Canton (and now transliterated as Huangpu), but in later years was known more simply as **Kowloon Docks**. Its opening was partly responsible for the rapid growth in Kowloon's population. For over a century, the docks built and overhauled ships of all kinds: from tea clippers to container ships. Indeed, any Star Ferry you have sailed upon probably bears a brass plaque recording its construction at Whampoa.

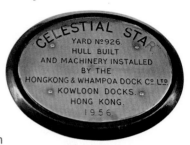

Shipbuilding has moved away from Hung Hom, but the dockyard's successor company, Hutchison Whampoa, still operates ports in Hong Kong and as far away as Panama and Felixstowe.

| *Berth certificate* |

| *Headquarters buildings of the Kowloon Docks* |

Machine shop: shipbuilding was Hong Kong's earliest heavy industry

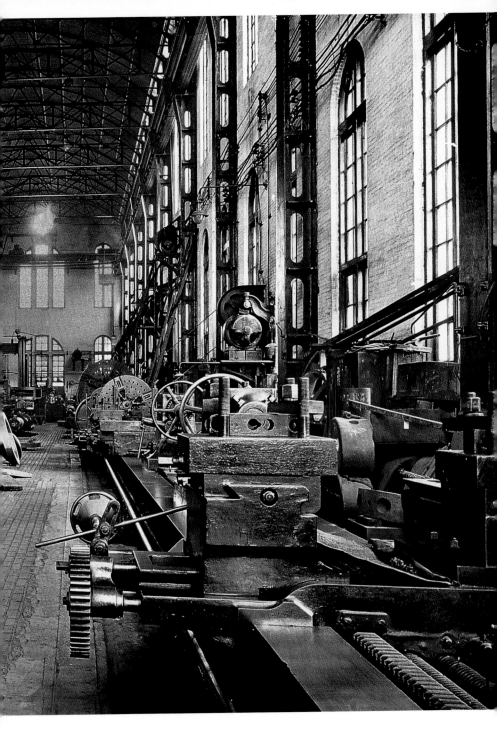

Turn left past the concrete ship onto Tak On Street, and follow it into an older part of Hung Hom. Kwun Yam Street leads up to Kowloon's most popular **temple to the Goddess of Mercy**. It was built in 1873 by the three local villages, and besides religious rites, its committee also provided education and medical care; services which were later taken up by the *kaifong* (neighbourhood association) which still has premises next door. The surrounding dockyards were a major target for bombing raids during World War II, but the temple remained unscathed, leading to tales of divine intervention. It's busy at most times but especially during Kwun Yam's four annual festivals.

Follow Station Lane back to Ma Tau Wai Road and turn left. You won't see many European faces in this part of town, but there is a large Indian community. By coincidence or otherwise, this district was also the location of the prisoner-of-war camp for Indian soldiers.

| At war's end, along with much of the city, the machine shop lay in ruins |

Kwun Yam temple

To Kwa Wan's 'tong lau' terraces

Palace of the Supreme Lord

The compact **Pak Tai temple** on the corner of Pak Kung Street was rebuilt here in 1929 after its small hilltop site was removed for roadbuilding. It's dedicated to the Supreme Lord of Dark Heaven, but there is also a local Earth god shrine in the courtyard. Turn into Bailey Street, named after another former dockyard, and then look for the second alley on your

Little Tokyo in Kowloon

right. Hidden at the end of an innocuous passage on the left is **Katiya Street**, a collection of Japanese eateries festooned with photogenic lanterns and cherry blossom. It's a popular destination for dinner.

A network of run-down old streets leads north from here to **Hoi Sham Park** on the waterfront. Take a look at the rocky hill and its pavilion. It was once an island in the harbour, but was joined to the mainland by reclamation in the 1960s. From here you can view the runway of the old Kai Tak airport.

Traces of the original shoreline

Lotus flower throne

Exiting the park, walk up Lok Shan Road, passing old-fashioned shops of all kinds. The Tin Hau temple on Ha Heung Road was built in 1885 by local Hakka fisherfolk. When Hoi Sham Island was reclaimed, a **temple to Lung Mo** (the Dragon Mother) was demolished, and the statue of the goddess was moved here to join Tin Hau. The temple's forecourt is attractively planted with bamboo and palm trees.

Many of the streets around here bear archaic names for Chinese provinces: Chi Kiang is Zhejiang, Kwei Chow is Guizhou, Sze Chuen is Sichuan, and so on. Carry on through the busy market area and follow Pau Chung Street until it too narrows into a fruit market. Turning right directly beforehand brings you to the somewhat unexpected sight of the **Ma Tau Kok Cattle Depot**.

This red-brick and green-tile slaughterhouse was built in 1908 and remained in use all the way until 1999, when it was renovated and converted into an artists' village. The compound is strangely reminiscent of a working-class English town of 50 years ago, and the impression is only reinforced by the circular tanks of a gasworks directly behind it. Not all of the artists' studios are open to the public, but there is usually at least one holding an exhibition – and you can peer into workshops occupied by such local creative personalities as the 'Frog King'.

On the far side of the gasworks, Kowloon City pier has ferry services back over the harbour to North Point. The last sailing is at 7:35 pm. If you miss it, tunnel bus 115 also runs across to Hong Kong Island.

Gasworks gallery:
outdoor installations
at the cattle depot

Wong Tai Sin to the Walled City

Wong Tai Sin ("Wong the great immortal") is one of Hong Kong's most popular gods, credited with granting many wishes. His temple in northeast Kowloon is one of the city's busiest. This walk also takes in Kowloon's last walled village, and the remains of the famous Walled City.

The walled compound of the Chinese magistrate's fort in 1865

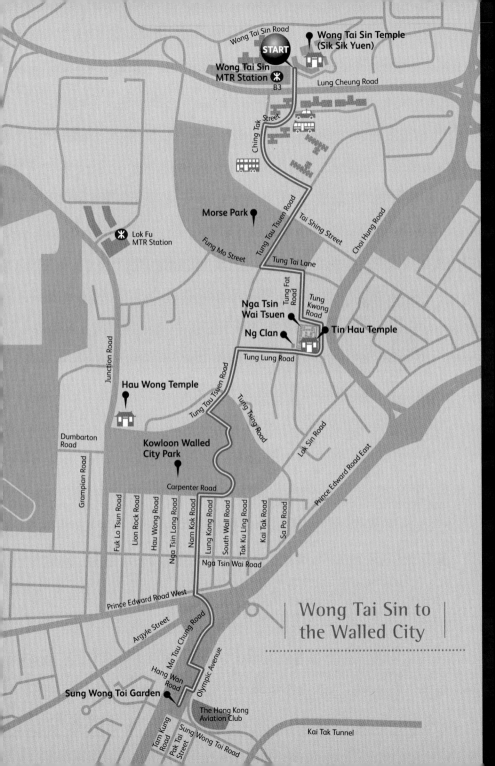

Wong Tai Sin to
the Walled City

Crowds of the faithful, clouds of incense

It couldn't be easier to find Wong's temple: simply take the MTR to **Wong Tai Sin**. Like Tin Hau on Hong Kong Island, the deity has given its name to the neighbourhood. Leave the station by Exit B3.

The Taoist god was originally a shepherd boy who was born in Zhejiang province at some time in the fourth century, but his cult only started to grow locally in 1915, when a portrait of him was brought from Guangdong and an altar dedicated in Wan Chai. The herbalist's shop which housed it burnt down shortly afterwards, and divinations suggested that a new site should be found at a certain distance inland from Kowloon City pier. This site was determined in 1921 on the then-remote foothills of Lion Rock.

The temple is always busy with worshippers and thick with incense smoke, and it's on a lot of tourist itineraries. It is a large compound with several halls, pleasant gardens, ponds and a nine-dragon wall which imitates one in Beijing's imperial palace. All five *feng shui* elements are represented: wood by the archive hall which contains books and scriptures; earth by the bricks in the wall; water by the fountain; fire by the shrine where incense is burned; and metal by the bronze pavilion, which is the only one of its kind in Hong Kong.

Taoist weddings are performed at the temple. A clinic offers Chinese medical treatment, some of it free of charge. There is also a 'soothsayers parade' with dozens of fortune tellers, some of whom can say sooths in English.

The organization which runs the complex, Sik Sik Yuen, came to an arrangement with the Tung Wah Hospital group in 1956 which allowed the temple to open its gates to the public and avoid redevelopment for housing. As part of the deal, Tung Wah was allowed to place a donation box at the entrance and collect the takings for charity. This arrangement remained unchallenged for over 50 years, but was brought into question by Sik Sik Yuen – which has since also evolved into a charitable institution, and therefore could also use the funds – in 2009.

| *Wong Tai Sin is credited with granting many wishes* |

To the right of the main gate, a 400-year-old horseshoe grave is maintained by the Lam clan, members of which built the important Tin Hau temple at Joss House Bay. A plaque installed by the clan records how ownership of the temple was taken from them by the government in 1938.

Passing the shops selling oranges, incense sticks, windmills and other devotional items, return to the main road and enter the shopping centre to cross the glass bridge. There's a taxi rank ahead of you. Turn right onto Ching Tak Street and follow it to its T-junction with Tung Tau Tsuen Road, where you should turn right again. This part of Kowloon can seem like one huge housing

Nga Tsin Wai: Kowloon's last walled village

estate, but at least the buildings are balanced by a lot of open green space. **Morse Park** on your right has Hong Kong's largest palm garden, with over 20 species of tropical palm trees. The park was also home to the historic pavilion of Blake Pier for many years, from when it was removed from the Central waterfront in 1965 until it was re-erected at Stanley in 2006.

Take the second left, Tung Tai Lane, and then turn right onto Tung Fat Road. This brings you to the ramshackle remnants of **Nga Tsin Wai**, the last walled village in Kowloon.

Enter by way of the main gate, in a small watchtower. In traditional fashion, this alley leads straight through the village to the early Qing-era **Tin Hau temple** at the back. Not many people still live in Nga Tsin Wai. Even though it has heritage potential – it dates back to the 13th century – the houses are gradually being bought by one of our esteemed tycoons, who demolishes each one as soon as he gains possession. For now, it is a reminder of what Kowloon was like before urbanization.

| Tin Hau temple |

| Offerings at the altar |

| Hall of the ancestors |

Pass the green-roofed ancestral hall of the **Ng clan** to return to Tung Tau Tsuen Road. Turning left brings you to the north gate of **Kowloon Walled City Park**.

The park, open from 6:30 am – 11:00 pm, was laid out in 1995 on the site of a historical anomaly. An imperial fort was built here at some point in the distant past, possibly to monitor the salt trade, and was expanded in the 1840s to keep an eye on the new British colony of Hong Kong across the harbour. A magistrate and garrison were stationed there. When Britain took over the New Territories in 1898, the fort fell within British territory, but a clause in the lease stated that China could keep an officer in the Walled City "to exercise jurisdiction except so far as may be inconsistent with the military requirements for the defence of Hongkong".

During 1899, the residing officer was found to be encouraging rebellion in the New Territories. He was expelled, and the clause in the treaty was revoked by the British. However, China continued to see the Walled City as a Chinese enclave within Hong Kong.

Fortress enclave: the original Walled City

Sir Alexander Grantham

The city walls were demolished during World War Two by the Japanese, to provide material for the extension of Kai Tak airport. The city degenerated into an overcrowded slum. In 1948, the Hong Kong authorities attempted to clear the area but were met by angry mobs who claimed that the city was Chinese territory. Riots spread to Guangzhou, where the British consulate was torched. Negotiations between Britain and the Kuomintang government of China brought no agreement, and the Walled City became a lawless no-man's-land. It was "a cesspool of iniquity, with heroin divans, brothels and everything unsavoury," according to **Sir Alexander Grantham**, governor in the 1950s, "for whilst we regularly sent in police patrols, we did not care to prosecute malefactors in the courts, lest the controversial issue of jurisdiction be raised by the defence".

Unlicensed dentist's surgery

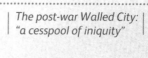

The post-war Walled City: "a cesspool of iniquity"

Standpipe in a darkened alley

Untouched by government,
the city grew upwards

Hidden by the high-rise slum, the Qing magistrate's office has been preserved

Unrestricted by any kind of zoning laws, and tapping electricity from the nearby estates, the city grew into a high-rise warren of dark alleyways, open sewers, drug dens, illicit dog meat restaurants and unlicensed dentists' surgeries. Children born there suffered from rickets due to lack of sunlight. The Hong Kong government again tried to intervene in 1962, only to receive a bizarre rebuke from the Communist authorities in support of the city's exploitative landlords – surely a running-dog rightist faction if ever there was one.

The matter was only settled in 1987, after agreement had been reached over Hong Kong's future as a whole. Both governments agreed that the city was in Hong Kong's jurisdiction and that it should be levelled. During demolition, the remnants of the original **Qing magistrate's office** – or 'yamen' – were found, along with fragments of the old south gate. They have been left in place in the park. The lintel of the yamen bears the English inscription 'Almshouse' – this was presumably its use after the magistrate was expelled in 1899.

Memories of Kai Tak: the Kowloon City flight path

On the south side of the park, the densely packed district of Kowloon City is well known for its Thai restaurants and groceries. The area is still mostly low-rise, a legacy of its close proximity to the old airport. Follow Nam Kok Road and take the underpass. A short way down Ma Tau Chung Road you'll find the small **Sung Wong Toi Garden**. The name means 'Terrace of the Sung Emperor' and recalls the two boy monarchs who were the last of their dynasty. Their travelling court spent some time in Kowloon, and on Lantau Island, in their flight from the invading Mongols at the end of the 13th century. The stone slab here inscribed with the three characters was originally part of a much larger rock, but the Japanese blew it up during the war (in common with the walls of Kowloon City)

Terrace of the Sung Emperor

to provide fill for expanding the airport. Luckily, the fragment of stone with the inscription survived, and was relocated here from its original small hill nearby.

The Hong Kong Aviation Club's hangar and clubhouse are located just over the road, in the grounds of the old airport. Since commercial flights were moved to Chek Lap Kok in 1998 and building height restrictions were relaxed, all small club aircraft have used the military airfield at Shek Kong instead. Club helicopters have continued to use the Kai Tak base, but since one of them crashed into a tour bus in early 2009, they are likely to be pressured to move out.

It's a good idea to return to Kowloon City and enjoy a Thai meal before catching a taxi back to the MTR. But if you're up for walking further, then take Junction Road north to Lok Fu. On the way you can visit the Hau Wong temple which is dedicated to Marquis Yeung, the loyal courtier of the two Sung emperors, who followed them to the last. There are other temples to his memory at Tai O and Tung Chung on Lantau, as described in the *Serious Hiker's Guide*.

Sham Shui Po

One of the older – and so far less redeveloped – districts of Kowloon, Sham Shui Po is most often visited for its street markets and computer malls. As a long-inhabited place, it has lots of character. This interesting urban walk also tells the story of Hong Kong's far-sighted postwar housing policy.

Leave Sham Shui Po MTR station by Exit C2 and turn left onto **Apliu Street**. It's one long open-air market, selling electrical items, hardware and household goods. The buildings date mostly from the 1960s, but look up and you'll occasionally see the upper floors of a shophouse which has somehow survived from the 1930s or earlier. Buildings of this era often had deep balconies to make the most of natural ventilation and shade.

Named for duck farms, Apliu Street is now a flea market

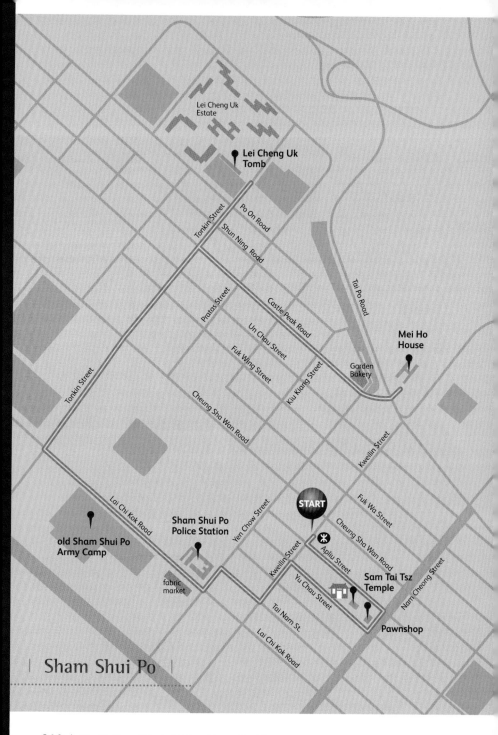

Lei Cheng Uk
Estate

**Lei Cheng Uk
Tomb**

Po On Road

Tonkin Street

Shun Ning Road

Tai Po Road

Pratas Street

Castle Peak Road

Un Chau Street

**Mei Ho
House**

Fuk Wing Street

Kiu Kiang Street

Garden
Bakery

Tonkin Street

Cheung Sha Wan Road

Kweilin Street

Yen Chow Street

START

Fuk Wa Street

Lai Chi Kok Road

**Sham Shui Po
Police Station**

Cheung Sha Wan Road

old Sham Shui Po
Army Camp

Kweilin Street

Apliu Street

Nam Cheong Street

**Sam Tai Tsz
Temple**

fabric
market

Yu Chau Street

Tai Nam St.

Lai Chi Kok Road

Pawnshop

Sham Shui Po

Panning for gold: trader sets out his wares

Pre-loved professional cameras

At the end of the street, a **photography shop** sells a great range of antique cameras, including defunct Russian and Chinese makes. Turn right and then right again. The corner of Nam Cheong Street is occupied by a **tall pawnshop**, a common feature in working-class districts. Consigned goods would have been kept under lock and key on the upper floors. The buildings beside it, which date from the 1920s and 1930s, have had their old balconies glassed in to create extra rooms inside – a result of the invention of air-conditioning and the constant pressure for living space in Hong Kong. Nevertheless, their pillared overhangs still protect pedestrians from rain and sun, an excellent system for our climate which has been ignored by modern architects.

A bat holding
a coin is the
emblem of a
pawnshop

Traditional shophouses: residential above, commercial below

A little way down Yu Chau Street, you'll find the **Sam Tai Tsz** temple. Dedicated to the obscure god Na Cha, otherwise known as the Third Prince, it's the only temple to him in Hong Kong. His legend is complicated but he is represented as a boy able to travel on wheels of fire. This temple was built by local Hakka people in 1898 to mark an outbreak of plague which was brought under control after an image of Na Cha had been brought here from Guangdong. There's also an altar inside to Pao Kung, the god of justice, and Kwun Yam, goddess of mercy.

Red-scarfed figurines sit in attendance

Temple of the Third Prince

Unchanged by the years, the station is a local landmark

The character of the area changes now to focus on clothing, with scores of small wholesale shops. It's not surprising, because the surrounding districts were long dominated by textile mills and garment factories. Turn left at the unusual corner shophouse – built in the 1920s and still bearing the stucco names of long-vanished businesses – onto busy Kweilin Street, a market of jade and food stalls. Tai Nan Street brings you to the attractive **Sham Shui Po Police Station**, built in 1924 on newly reclaimed land. It is still used for its original purpose.

Shophouse on the corner

The camp housed an increased British garrison after the General Strike of 1925

Over the intersection there's another fabric market, this time covered but scruffy and proclaimed a 'hawker bazaar'. The park beyond it on Lai Chi Kok Road occupies part of the site of the **old Sham Shui Po army camp** which was laid out in the 1920s. After the Japanese invasion, it was converted into a prisoner-of-war camp for Allied soldiers, and the police station was used as its command post. It was returned to the British Army after the war, and was later used to house Vietnamese

Remembering the prisoners of war

boat people. None of the military buildings remain, but plaques have been erected in memory of its wartime role, and maple trees have been planted to remember the Canadian soldiers who were imprisoned here.

Tonkin Street is the most direct route to Lei Cheng Uk Estate. Here, set into a small but pleasant park, is one of Hong Kong's true antiquities: a large and **ancient tomb** which was discovered by accident in 1955 when workmen were levelling the hillside to make way for new buildings. Its four domed chambers, arranged in a cross shape, are made of brick. A wealth of bronze and ceramic relics were found within, thought to date from the Han Dynasty (25-220 AD). The site is open every day except Thursdays.

Cruciform tomb: Lei Cheng Uk

Walking down Castle Peak Road will take you past the Garden Bakery, where most of Hong Kong's bread and biscuits are made. On the other side of Tai Po Road, the stark **Mei Ho House** – or 'Block 41' – has survived the demolition of the Shek Kip Mei Estate to stand as a reminder of Hong Kong's post-war migration problems and housing policy.

The estate was built as an emergency response to the devastating Shek Kip Mei squatter hut fire of 1953 (following spread), which left tens of thousands of hillside dwellers homeless overnight. At the time, Hong Kong was being swamped by yet another wave of refugees from the mainland. These new migrants, fleeing the Communist takeover of China, were housed in 'cottage areas' of self-built shacks which covered hillsides beside every urban part of Hong Kong Island and Kowloon.

The fire began on Christmas Day, in a hut which served as both a home and workshop, when an unwatched kerosene stove was tipped over. Within minutes, wooden walls were ablaze. Fanned by a strong wind, the flames erupted into a firestorm. Within hours 53,000 people were homeless.

| Mei Ho House |

The first resettlement blocks were built in Shek Kip Mei

Squatters' rights: Hong Kong's hillsides were covered with refugee huts

An unattended stove sparked a blaze which engulfed the settlement

*Safe from the flames,
but refugees once more*

*The fire destroyed the homes
of over 50,000 people*

Communal living: the
Hong Kong experience

The event forced the government to face the problem of the quickly mounting population. A decision was made to embark on a vast construction programme of multi-storey **resettlement estates,** and Shek Kip Mei was the testing ground. A total of 29 utilitarian H-shaped blocks were built to house the former squatter families. Each six- or seven-storey block had communal toilets and standpipes. Residents had to cook in the corridors, and school classes were held on rooftops. Mobile libraries visited the busy outdoor market streets below. A unit of barely 100 square feet had to house a whole extended family. Conditions were extremely basic, but this project was the birth of the public housing scheme which turned the Hong Kong Government, nominally the overseer of the world's freest economy, into the world's biggest landlord. Today, over two million people live in much-improved government housing.

A large portion of Hong Kong's post-war generation grew up in the resettlement blocks. A much-loved RTHK television drama, *Below Lion Rock,* caught the essence of those times by depicting the neighbourliness of the crowded estates – a warmth which is not seen so often in modern developments.

Mei Ho House is being converted into a youth hostel, and will include a museum showcasing this poverty-stricken – but upwardly mobile – period of Hong Kong's recent history. Kweilin Street is your quickest route back to the MTR.

Gin Drinkers' Line and the Shing Mun Redoubt

Hong Kong's own version of the Maginot Line – a fortified boundary north of Kowloon intended to halt the advance of enemy troops – never had any real chance of success. In 1941, it fell to the Japanese in just two days. Today you can follow sections of the Maclehose Trail to visit the remains of bunkers and pillboxes on the Gin Drinkers' Line. This reasonably challenging hike is an all-day affair but will reward you at its highest points with almost-aerial views of Kowloon.

Up until the 1920s, Britain had invested a lot in the colony's defences, but these were all aimed at keeping foreign naval powers (primarily Russia and France) at bay. China was never seen as a threat and so the land border was never fortified. The situation changed with Japan's full-scale invasion of China in 1937, and despite the prevailing beliefs that Japan could never defeat a Western power, efforts were made to construct an east-west defensive line across the peaks surrounding Kowloon. The name was not intended to reflect the off-duty habits of British officers; instead, it was named after Gin Drinkers' Bay at its western point, now long buried under reclamation. The line included a commanding redoubt at Shing Mun.

Kowloon from the heights of Lion Rock

Wartime allies: Churchill, Roosevelt and Chiang Kai-shek

As the drums of war began to beat louder in 1939, conscription for European males was announced in Hong Kong and women and children were evacuated to Australia. British prime minister **Winston Churchill** had no illusions. "If Japan goes to war with us there is not the slightest chance of holding Hong Kong or relieving it," he wrote. "It is most unwise to increase the loss we shall suffer there. Instead of increasing the garrison it ought to be reduced to a symbolical scale."

So it was that two battalions of untested Canadian recruits arrived in late 1941, to join British, Indian and local soldiers in facing a battle-hardened Japanese force which had proved its mettle in China. The result was predictable but nevertheless tragic.

Encampment in the hills

Doomed defenders of Hong Kong

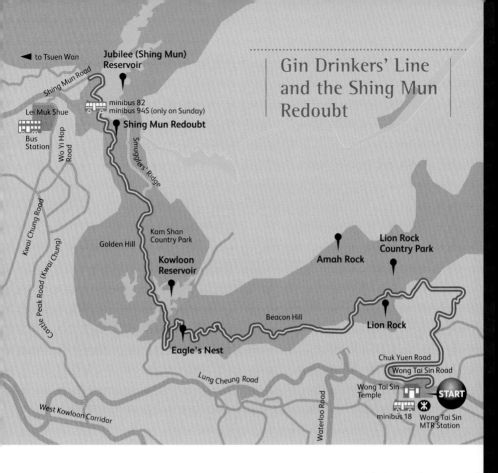

to Tsuen Wan ◄

Shing Mun Road

Jubilee (Shing Mun) Reservoir

Lei Muk Shue

Wo Yi Hop Road

Bus Station

minibus 82
minibus 94S (only on Sunday)

Shing Mun Redoubt

Smugglers' Ridge

Kwai Chung Road

Castle Peak Road (Kwai Chung)

Golden Hill

Kam Shan Country Park

Kowloon Reservoir

Amah Rock

Lion Rock Country Park

Beacon Hill

Lion Rock

Eagle's Nest

Lung Cheung Road

West Kowloon Corridor

Waterloo Road

Chuk Yuen Road

Wong Tai Sin Road

Wong Tai Sin Temple

minibus 18

Wong Tai Sin MTR Station

START

Gin Drinkers' Line and the Shing Mun Redoubt

From Wong Tai Sin MTR, take a taxi (or green minibus 18 and a 30-minute walk uphill) to Sha Tin Pass. The trail starts at the last hairpin bend before the village café, at the entrance to **Lion Rock Country Park**. A quick climb leads to an easy ridge path with views of Kowloon and Hong Kong Island through the trees. You'll soon see the first of several military distance markers. An information board recounts the findings of **Lt Col Lindsay Ride** that these signs revealed pillbox locations to the enemy; but this was hardly necessary, for the Japanese had run an extensive intelligence network in Hong Kong before the war and their officers carried detailed maps of British positions.

Lt Col Lindsay Ride

| Lion Rock Country Park | | Forest walk high above the city |

The local landmark of **Amah Rock** can be seen to the north. The legend connected to it dates from the Sung dynasty. A soldier in the retinue of the Emperor had to flee the invading Mongols, leaving his wife and newborn baby to fend for themselves. The woman roamed the hills collecting firewood with her baby on her back, looking out to sea for her husband's return. Eventually she was transformed into the standing stone you see today.

A side path leads up to the double summit of Lion Rock – take the detour if you have no fear of heights. The main trail crosses Kowloon Pass onto an open hillside with lovely views of Lion Rock and Kowloon Peak behind you. A service road leads to the top of Beacon Hill, where fires were once lit to signal danger. Descend by way of the path which crosses the road several more times. The Maclehose skirts Eagle's Nest and then runs downhill to Tai Po Road, the old main route into the New Territories, where aggressive macaques hang around (literally) hoping to get food from visitors.

Military markers still in place

Crafty macaques cadge for crumbs

Indian troops bolstered
Hong Kong's defences

Serpentine stretch
of the Kowloon
reservoirs

Excavating tunnels beneath Smuggler's Ridge

Cross the road and bear right to pick up the trail on the other side: it enters Kam Shan ("Gold Mountain") Country Park and crosses the curved dam of the **Kowloon Reservoir**. When built in 1910, this was the largest reservoir in Hong Kong. In order to fill it, a village in the valley had to be relocated to Sha Tin. The dam formed part of the withdrawal route of British troops.

The road leads up into thickly wooded hills, perfect habitat for the macaques. At a fork in the trail, turn left. The route then leaves the road to head along a hill path parallel to Smugglers' Ridge.

You now approach the ruins of the **Shing Mun Redoubt**. The underground system of tunnels, pillboxes and lookout posts had clear views of the approaches to Kowloon, but its design was fatally flawed: ventilation shafts were uncovered, allowing attackers to drop grenades into them. This was compounded by a severe lack of manpower which meant that the Royal Scots could not mount effective foot patrols outside the fort.

Underground, a citadel for homesick British soldiers

| Directions from past and present |

Unguarded entrance to the Shing Mun Redoubt

Stairway into subterranean chambers

The Japanese 228th Regiment crossed the border into Hong Kong on the 8th of December 1941, to no resistance, and reached Shing Mun the next day. Road bridges in the New Territories had been blown up to delay them, but the Japanese advanced on foot, using village paths.

It had been clear from as early as the 1930s that the Gin Drinkers' Line was untenable – it required six battalions to man it, but only three were available. The aim instead was to slow the Japanese advance by a week or so and inflict casualties on the attackers, but even this proved impossible: the redoubt was taken, the line was compromised in just two days and Commonwealth forces were forced to retreat to Hong Kong Island, crossing the harbour at Devil's Peak.

The ruins are in reasonably good condition and can be explored if you bring a torch. Tunnels leading into the complex are marked 'Regent Street', 'Charing Cross' and so on, London placenames familiar to the Middlesex Regiment which built them. Japanese inscriptions are also carved into the walls. A local

Hong Kong could not escape a world at war

walkers' group has posted notices asking visitors to respect the sacrifices made here by soldiers of all nationalities.

The name 'Shing Mun' means 'city gate' and recalls a much earlier fort built on this site by Ming loyalists in the 17th century. Carry on downhill to a barbecue site beside Jubilee Reservoir, named for the silver jubilee of King George V in 1935. The great bulk of Tai Mo Shan, the highest point in Hong Kong, sits to the north. Turn left to reach Pineapple Dam, which recalls the fruits grown by the former Hakka villagers of the valley. Starting in 1862, a three-year 'village war' took place between the pineapple farmers of Shing Mun and the market traders of Tsuen Wan, resulting in 34 fatalities.

Green minibus 82 (and the 94S on Sundays) runs from the visitor centre down into Tsuen Wan, where you can rejoin the MTR; or you can walk down Shing Mun Road to the bus terminus at Lei Muk Shue. If you still have time, you can visit Sam Tung Uk, a Hakka walled village near Tsuen Wan MTR station which is now run as a folk museum.

Tai Po and Kam Tin

When Britain took control of the New Territories in early 1899, it promised to respect the traditional customs of the mostly rural populations which had lived there for centuries. But this policy didn't mollify every villager – some took up arms against the invaders, and the handover was not entirely peaceful. After a brief conflict, the market town of Tai Po became the centre of government for the area. This excursion takes in some vestiges of its Victorian past, and also visits some of the villages which resisted British rule.

Take the MTR, formerly KCR, to Tai Po Market station and leave by the exit for Uptown Plaza. Bear right and follow the covered walkway past the green taxis, turning immediately right again to take an underpass under the railway line.

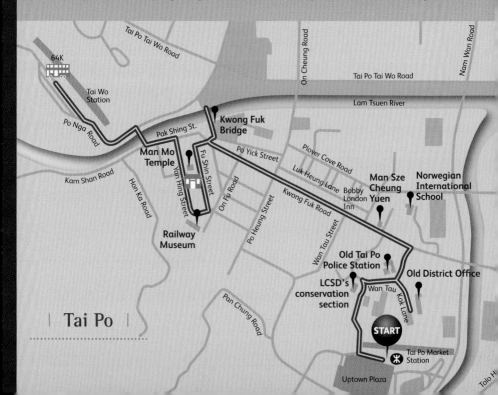

Colonial command post: the Old Tai Po Police Station

A traditional *pai lau* gateway, dated 1953, bids you welcome to Tai Po Primary School. The school is long gone, but its grounds have been transformed into gardens where mature residents perform *tai chi* moves under mature trees.

| Tai chi under the trees |

The old pitched-roof buildings below the garden as you exit, originally government quarters, are now used as offices for the **LCSD's conservation section**. Turn right onto Wan Tau Kok Lane and carry on uphill.

The low buildings in the fenced compound on your left were the premises of the **Old Tai Po Police Station**, the very first in the New Territories. They were

| Flagstaff Hill |

built in 1899. It was probably here on Flagstaff Hill, on April 17th of that year, that Governor Sir Henry Blake officiated at a flag-raising ceremony to mark the addition of the New Territories to Hong Kong. The hill was then nearer the coast of Tolo Harbour and provided a splendid vantage point for governing this new dominion. Indian soldiers from the Hong Kong Regiment stood in attendance along with marines and sailors from HMS *Fame*.

Britain needed the extra land to defend Victoria Harbour not from China but from the territorial ambitions of other European naval powers; France had recently been granted a port at what is now Zhanjiang, Russia was installed at Port Arthur, and Germany had

New Territories: Blake raises the flag on Hong Kong's new lands

colonized Qingdao. In the weeks before the flag-raising event at Tai Po, however, a rebellion took place across what had previously been known as Sun On county. No one had asked the farmers and fishermen whether they wanted to become part of Hong Kong, and many had been given no warning of the impending change. Some violently objected to the idea. When the Captain Superintendent of Police, Francis Henry May, arrived at Tai Po on the 3rd of April to inspect the temporary police matsheds, he was met with a barrage of stones hurled by the local inhabitants. That evening, the matsheds were razed to the ground by angry villagers, and May was forced to beat a hasty retreat.

The five main clans of the New Territories were used to fighting each other, and they quickly raised an army to attack the colonialists. Possibly the lightly-armed militiamen didn't know they were taking on the British Empire at the height of its power.

Six-day war: the Fusiliers with field gun

Among the units sent to quell the uprising were the **Royal Welch Fusiliers**. Soldiers of this regiment wore five black silk ribbons on the nape of their jacket collars, a relic of the time when it was customary for soldiers to wear their hair in plaits. The fighting was over in six days, with heavy casualties on the Chinese side.

Blake was keen to build a more cordial relationship with the pacified clans, and he arranged meetings with groups of village elders to explain British intentions. He met the Sai Kung and Kowloon representatives near the Kowloon Walled City in April, and the Tai Po and Yuen Long elders separately in August. This last meeting took place in **Ping Shan**, in a Tang clan ancestral hall which still stands. Blake took pains to appear conciliatory – he was accompanied only by policemen and an honour guard of two or three soldiers.

The full extent of both Deep Bay and Mirs Bay were included in the lease of the New Territories, preventing Chinese customs boats from collecting revenues in those waters. This is why the far-off island of Tung Ping Chau is part of Hong Kong today. The land border followed the Sham Chun (Shenzhen) River, a poor choice which allowed easy smuggling; a proposal to draw the border along the mountain ridge to the north was rejected. British

Governor Blake meets the clan elders

Victory over the villages

troops nevertheless occupied Sham Chun for a few months before withdrawing south of the river.

The Old Tai Po Police Station served its original purpose until 1987, and was last used as temporary accommodation for the Marine Police – hence the standard-issue blue and white paint – but now awaits further use. At present you cannot enter, but the site is set to be converted into an education centre by Kadoorie Farm. Perhaps a commemorative flagstaff could be re-erected at some point.

Hilltop verandah

Market town walk-ups

Further up the road, the elegant colonial structure cresting the hill is the **Old District Office**. Dating from 1907, the red-brick building has cooling verandahs along two sides. All the early development of the northern New Territories – mapping, reclamation, and the construction of railways, roads and reservoirs – was planned from here by multi-tasking district officers. It remained in use until 1983, and is now occupied by the Scout Association of Hong Kong.

If you walk around the building, you can return downhill by a different set of steps through lush tropical foliage. Turn right at the old police station to descend through the trees to Kwong Fuk Road.

Before the development of the new town and the Tolo Highway, Kwong Fuk Road was the main thoroughfare of Tai Po – a continuation of the old Tai Po Road, which winds its way around the hillsides from Kowloon towards the border. Groom's Cottage, the brick building on the other side of the road, was either stables or servants' quarters for the Old Police Bungalow on the hill above it. The bungalow was built in 1909 and housed four single police officers. In those days, before reclamation of the shoreline, the hillock would have been surrounded by marshy land. The bungalow is now occupied by the Norwegian International School.

Man Sze Cheung Yuen, the low-rise balconied house facing Groom's Cottage, comes straight out of 1960s Hong Kong. It has a walled orchard behind it. Even in villages, it's rare to find this amount of open space attached to a house.

| Kwong Fuk Bridge | | Covered crossing |

Carry on along Kwong Fuk Road, passing the Bobby London Inn which has been quenching the thirst of policemen and other Tai Po expats for the past thirty years. Luk Heung Lane, which runs parallel, is named after the six villages which were submerged beneath the waters of the Plover Cove Reservoir in the 1960s; the former villagers were resettled here.

The end of Kwong Fuk Road is marked by a line of old walk-up buildings very characteristic of urban back streets; vertical vents let air and light into the central stairwell, bringing to mind an old-fashioned radio set. Past these, the **Kwong Fuk Bridge** crosses the Lam Tsuen River. A foundation stone is inscribed with the year 1957, but this probably refers to an older bridge on the site, for it was once a busy vehicle crossing. The present bridge is a 'dual carriageway' – bicycles on one side and pedestrians on the other.

Turn back and cross the road to find a van parking area. Turning directly left behind it puts you on the narrow Fu Shin Street, a great example of a bustling street market. All kinds of fresh produce are noisily bought and sold. Old-style shops sell dried seafood, Chinese herbs, traditional sweets and religious paraphernalia. Designed before the advent of cars changed the urban landscape, human-scale streets like this help to make towns liveable.

| Shopping alfresco |

| Temple in the market |

Halfway down you'll find the attractive **Man Mo Temple**, set in a small garden. Unspoilt by heavy-handed restoration, it looks its age. It's dedicated to the same gods of literature and war as the temple on Hollywood Road and was built in 1891. The market dates from the same time. The local rural committee used one room inside to arbitrate on weights and measures, to ensure the fairness of market trading.

Turn right at the end of the street. **The Railway Museum** is straight ahead. Built in 1913 as the Kowloon-Canton Railway station for Tai Po Market, it was the only station on the line designed in Chinese style. It has been out of use since electrification of the line in 1983, and now operates as an open-

| Edwardian engines: the Kowloon-Canton Railway |

air exhibition. You can board old carriages, look around the ticket office and see the old steam locomotive. The museum is open until 5:00 pm every day except Tuesday.

Follow Yan Hing Street and turn left to cross the river. Today, it is a carefully channelled waterway, but try to imagine it at the turn of the century, when thousands of Hoklo boat people lived on sampans in the estuary. Turn left again to reach Tai Wo train station, at which point you can finish your walk. Or alternatively, jump on bus 64K on the left-hand side of the bus station to travel on to Kam Tin.

Take a seat upstairs. The bus follows the river upstream into the Lam Tsuen Valley, site of the locally famous **Wishing Tree**, a banyan laden with hundreds of oranges thrown up into its

| Steam power |

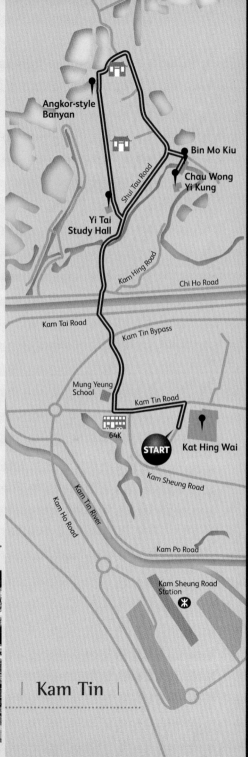

Angkor-style Banyan

Bin Mo Kiu

Chau Wong Yi Kung

Shui Tau Road

Yi Tai Study Hall

Kam Hing Road

Chi Ho Road

Kam Tai Road

Kam Tin Bypass

Mung Yeung School

Kam Tin Road

64K

START   Kat Hing Wai

Kam Sheung Road

Kam Tin River

Kam Ho Road

Kam Po Road

Kam Sheung Road Station

| Kam Tin |

Weighted wishes in the boughs

branches in the hope of having wishes granted. Look out for it on your right. On the left, the forested slopes of Tai Mo Shan hide the steep Ng Tung Chai waterfalls. For the most part it's a pleasingly rural scene, and at least as you approach the higher reaches, you can appreciate the words of Graham Heywood, who wrote in 1938: "The hills stand around the valley, shutting it off from the busy world outside, and the villages and fields and woods have an air of immemorial calm; here, more than anywhere else in the New Territories, you will be enfolded in the deep peace of the countryside."

As you reach the highest point of the road, Kadoorie Farm and Botanic Garden appears on your left, rising in terraces up the side of Kwun Yam Shan. Founded in 1956 to provide self-help aid to farmers who had come to Hong Kong as destitute refugees, today it promotes organic agriculture and the conservation of biodiversity in Hong Kong and southern China. The idea came to Sir Horace Kadoorie when he discovered a tangerine tree growing on the upper slopes of Tai Mo Shan. At the time, general opinion was that citrus fruits could not flourish in the high altitude, humidity and steep terrain of Hong Kong's hills, but the tangerine tree found growing untended and unwatered was proof that they could. You can explore the Farm; it's open daily until 5:00 pm.

The road drops downhill now towards the Pat Heung ('Eight Villages') valley, centred on the Shek Kong airstrip. The Royal Air Force based themselves here from the 1950s onwards, and it is now used by the People's Liberation Army Air Force. An obelisk beside the road at Sheung Tsuen looks old but actually commemorates the 1997 handover.

The bus makes a big loop south around the airfield, giving you glimpses of temples and ancestral halls surviving among the three-storey villas and breakers' yards which now scatter the plain. 'Indigenous' New Territories villagers – those who can trace their lineage to one of the recognized villages of 1898 – still occupy a privileged position in Hong Kong society, and are left largely to govern themselves. Since 1972, each male villager over the age of 18 can apply for a plot of government land on which to build a house. This policy was introduced as a temporary measure to keep farming communities alive, but has outlasted its purpose and is now a licence to print money; the right to build these houses is often pre-sold to developers. The major problem is that this kind of development is unplanned, paying no attention to water, power or transport links, and has blighted much of the flat land of the New Territories. The anachronistic policy should be rescinded, but the Heung Yee Kuk, the villagers' powerful lobby group, has seats in the Legislative Council and seems to have a veto over any government decisions.

The bus pulls in briefly to Kam Sheung West Rail station and then returns to cross a river. Get off a few stops later, after the bus has turned left onto Kam Tin Road. Walk back along the road. Kam Tin is a rather scrappy town, but you don't need to walk through too much of it to reach **Kat Hing Wai**.

Grey-brick antiquities

A *wai* is a walled village, and Kam Tin is famous for having a large number of them, built by branches of the Tang clan. The prosperous Tangs arrived in the area over 500 years ago, during the Ming dynasty, and founded multiple settlements in Kam Tin, Ping Shan and Fanling. The walls of Kat Hing Wai are well preserved, and they still work: you will have to pay the old ladies of the village if you wish to enter.

Governor Stubbs at the return of the gates to Kat Hing Wai

Modern-day residents remember Reginald

Take a look at the fine iron gates at the entrance. In retaliation for the villagers' refusal to open them in 1899, they were carted off as trophies by the British troops. The British also seized the gates of Tai Hong Wai just to the north, and blew down the walls on either side for good measure. One half of each set of gates was damaged by generations of village pigs using them as scratching posts, but Sir Henry Blake combined the other halves and sent the good pair back to his country estate in Ireland. There they remained as a garden feature until 1925, when a petition for their return was successful. The governor of the day, **Sir Reginald Stubbs**, was keen to secure good relations with the Chinese, and when the gates were restored he travelled to Kam Tin to pose for a photograph with the village elders.

You can make a circular tour of other Tang-built antiquities in the area. Walk back down Kam Tin Road and turn right in front of Mung Yeung School, and then follow the track north across the bypass and river channel. At a fork in the road, a sign above some bins points you in either direction. Turn left to find the nicely renovated **Yi Tai Study Hall**. This was built in the 19th century as a place for local boys to study for the imperial examinations – success in these ensured high status in life.

| Imperial study hall |

For mother's convenience

Carrying on north through Shui Tau takes you past a succession of imposing temples and ancestral halls, and a great banyan tree wrapped around the remains of a stone house, until you reach a Tin Hau temple beside fishponds. Turn right here to follow the road back south, and then make a left turn at a red post. A path leads to the **Bin Mo Kiu**, or Bridge for Mother's Convenience, built by a dutiful son in 1710 to allow his mother to cross the stream to visit her grandchildren. Apparently it took him six years to save the money to build it, and his act of filial piety was held up as an example for village children for generations afterwards.

Crossing the stone slabs of the bridge, you'll find the **Chau Wong Yi Kung**, a hall built in 1685 in honour of the two Qing officials who convinced the Emperor to reverse the coastal evacuation order of 1662. This edict, intended to deprive seaborne Ming rebels of supplies, was disastrous for coastal residents, including those of the New Territories. Deprived of their means of livelihood, many who were forced to relocate inland starved there. Chau and Wong were therefore held in high regard by the people who were able to return.

The impressive Angkor-style **banyan tree** you saw earlier could well be connected to this period of history. It may have started growing beside the stone house when its inhabitants were evacuated far inland, and during their exile, its aerial roots began to wrap themselves around the walls and lintels. Since the owners never returned, there was no one to stop the house falling down, but the great tree has preserved its outline.

Carry on in the same direction to return to the new river channel, and cross it by any of the bridges to return through village areas to the main road. Besides the descendants of the Tangs, Kam Tin today also has a very visible Nepalese population, a legacy of the Gurkha units which served here in the British Army.

You can make your way back to the Kam Sheung MTR station by foot, bus or taxi; or, for a more interesting route back to town, take bus 51, which climbs up the sides of Tai Mo Shan on its way over to Tsuen Wan.

Family tree: the house-hugging banyan

Acknowledgments

Source of Images

FormAsia is grateful to the following individuals and institutions for the assistance provided by enabling it to obtain key photographs of events and locations that would otherwise have been inaccessible.

Please accept our sincere thanks.

The Peak
Alumni Office – University of Hong Kong
Information Services Department, HKSAR
Bob Davis – Photographer, Hong Kong
Dennis George Crow, New York
Picture This Ltd., Hong Kong

Bowen to Barker
David Mahoney, West Sussex, The United Kingdom

Hong Kong University & Sai Ying Pun
Swiss Evangelic Mission, Archives Mission 21, Zurich
National Diet Library, Tokyo
Pasteur Institute, Paris

Pok Fu Lam
Time/Life Images, New York

Sheung Wan & Hollywood Road
Queen's College, Leung Wai-shun – Assistant Principal

Around the Escalator
Andrew E. Tse
Laura De Costa Roque – Miss Hong Kong, 1967

Around Victoria Barracks
Mrs Betty Simpson, General Manager – The Helena May
Dr. Elizabeth Profit, Chairman of the Helena May Library Committee
Andrew Seaton – The British Consul General
Russel Middleton, Regional Overseas Security Manager – The British Consulate-General, Hong Kong
University of British Columbia – Asian Library, Canada

Central
Page 190, The South China Morning Post

Wong Nai Chung Gap
Darlene and Ronaldo Parker, Ontario, Canada
State Library of Victoria, Melbourne, Australia
The Australian War Memorial, Canberra, Australia

Quarry Bay
Maisie Shun Wah – John Swire & Sons (H.K.) Ltd.
Robert Jennings – John Swire & Sons Ltd.

Stanley
Jamie Cox
Geoff Emerson
Joyce Ho, Officer – Correctional Services Department
Fr. Brian Barrons M.M. – Maryknoll Mission
Ellen Pierce, Director – Maryknoll Mission, New York

Tsim Sha Tsui
Lynn Edwards: Head of Security, IFCII

Hung Hom & Harbour Ferries
W.H. Lam: Wong & Ouyang Architects

Wong Tai Sin to the Walled City
Ian Lambot: Photographer & Publisher of *The City Of Darkness*

Sham Shui Po
Barry W. Jones, Secretary – The Royal Hong Kong Police Association, London

Tai Po & Kam Tin
Dr Patrick Hase